SO GREAT A HERITAGE

★ ★ ★ ★ ★

by
KATHIE JACKSON

Tate Publishing, LLC.

DEDICATION

★ ★ ★ ★ ★

This book is dedicated to my father plus the thousands that fought to defend our country and continue to defy the enemies of freedom.

Also

To the God of Truth who conquers darkness even in our bleakest moments--for His guidance and Peace in my life.

"To you, O Lord, I lift up my soul.
O my God, I trust in You"
Psalm 25:1 (NKJV)

ACKNOWLEDGEMENTS

★ ★ ★ ★ ★

Viki, Eddie, and Terri—for helping me gather all of our father's letters and photos.

Rebekah and April—for hours at the keyboard entering their grandfather's letters into the computer and proofreading.

Brian Schenk, Librarian and Archivist, Texas Military Forces Museum—for giving me so much time and information, and pointing me in the right direction.

Pam Robertson—for her work as my "Punctuation Nazi."

Summer Leigh—for helping her Aunt Kathie edit.

Nelda Laney—for her encouragement and editing.

Louise Harper—for her excitement and advice.

Donice Johnson—for her help with the cover photo.

Lieutenant General Carl E. Franklin USAF (Retired)—for his expertise and encouragement.

My sweet Michael—for his encouragement and faith in me.

TABLE OF CONTENTS

★ ★ ★ ★ ★

AUTHOR'S NOTE 9

INTRODUCTION 11

CHAPTER 1 Training Camps 17

CHAPTER 2 North Africa 41

CHAPTER 3 Italy 79

CHAPTER 4 France 171

CHAPTER 5 Germany 265

EPILOGUE 325

CREDITS 341

AUTHOR'S NOTE

★ ★ ★ ★ ★

Only be careful, and watch yourselves closely so that you do not forget the things your eyes have seen or let them slip from your heart as long as you live. Teach them to your children and to their children after them.

Deuteronomy 4:9 (NIV)

We live in a time when many people do not know who they are. I teach adolescents who are struggling to discover themselves as they break more and more ties with their parents. The happier and more mature teenagers are the ones who have discovered that rejection of their family is to reject themselves. They are the product—like it or not—of parents who not only conceived them, but also provide them the life they enjoy. Accepting who they are while learning from their parents' mistakes is the purest definition of growth. Those who never embrace their heritage are destined to live with an emptiness that eats away precious years.

Such is our nation today. Gone are the years when, like little boys bragging on their fathers, we were not embarrassed to celebrate our nation's incredible Christian heritage. As we travel deeper into the 21st century however, our older nation struggles through an identity crisis. Embarrassed at times with the God of our ancestors, we try to rewrite history to make ourselves not sound so fanatical—more "politically correct." Just as teenagers tend to blow-off the sacrifices their parents have made and blow up their imperfections, page after page has been written in recent years to villainize the motives and morals of our forefathers.

Combined with this disturbing climate of rewriting our past is a genuine lack of first-hand knowledge of contemporary heroes. We are stacking up generations of Americans who have never known anyone who risked their life on a battlefield. War stories remain merely words in a history textbook that will never touch deeply until we have a personal connection with these brave soldiers. Without a vision of what real people gave up and endured, conflicts and battles are just headings on a page . . . and those who fought them are just a number among many.

My desire is for my children to know where they came from and who they need to thank for the blessings they enjoy today. By opening a window to the past, perhaps they can relive the danger, cold, and loneliness their grandfather endured and catch a glimpse of the faith that sustained him. My prayer is that you, the reader, will also connect with him—someone you have never met before. Talented fiction authors are able to draw you into lives of those who never existed. The real people in these pages had busy lives an insane dictator interrupted and disturbed. Unlike many historical works, nothing in these pages has been changed to protect the innocent. In fact, the truth should enlighten them and "set them free."

INTRODUCTION

★ ★ ★ ★ ★

But you must continue in the things which you have learned and been assured of, knowing from whom you have learned them, and that from childhood you have known the Holy Scriptures, which are able to make you wise for salvation through faith which is in Christ Jesus.

2 Timothy 3:14–15 (NKJV)

When we sold my parents' house, we discovered the "treasure." My mother lived in a nearby nursing home for years, and we finally decided it was time to sell the family home. My brother, sisters and I set aside a few days to try to sort and distribute the "stuff" left behind after a lifetime. I am blessed with incredible siblings, so the days were filled with tears not from quarrelling, but from laughter and memories of days spent in the wonderful Christian home my parents provided for all four of us. It was on the second day of digging and sorting that we discovered the "treasure." We spent days going through closets and cabinets and finally came to a cedar chest which had been locked to our little fingers while growing up. We found baby books and other wonderful mementos plus a mysterious, large scrapbook. None could remember ever seeing the homemade wooden cover before that day. Heavy cords passed through carefully drilled holes and held the handcrafted boards together. Pressed between the wood was a large stack of black sheets. Page after page had photographs and thick envelopes arranged and carefully mounted. We had discovered a stash of letters and photos from our father to his parents during World War II. With so much left to sift through, time pressured us to divide the letters and photos quickly and go on to the next project.

Not many days after returning home, the box of letters drew me. Each "V-Mail" transported me back to the war-torn 1940s. I sat there for hours as the personal yet historical significance sunk in. My children avoided me so they would not be subjected once again to my sob-filled attempts to read another of their granddad's letters aloud. Within a week, I had heard from my brother and two sisters who were equally awestruck with the discovery. The faint and faded letters narrated four years of our father's life and the ink captured the epic struggle of our nation, unaffected by time. Glimpses into the thoughts and dreams of this young man were a great gift from God. The treasure revealed a facet of our dad's life we never knew and the relationship with his parents and family we barely knew.

My father died of cancer in 1986, just 6 weeks after my youngest child was born. He was not a perfect man, but I have yet to meet someone I would rather have had for my father. Sometimes when I see him in a photo or on video, the pain of loss still grabs my heart. My fondest memories were the occasions I had him all to myself. Occasionally I was the only one playing in the front yard and heard him honk on the way to the cotton gin with a trailer piled high with cotton. I would climb up beside him and snuggle close to the man I could proudly call "Daddy."

How Dad loved being a farmer. To him, the land was an artist's fresh canvas and held so many possibilities. He began each season with prayer and ended the harvest with praise to his God. My favorite quote came when he was busily preparing the fields for the next stage. "We need to get in a position for God to bless us." These images of him on the farm were my first and almost last ones as well. Before the cancer confined him to bed, he continued to drive out and survey the land he had plowed, sweated, and prayed over most of his life. Death took my father before I realized this love of farming sprouted early in him as the youngest son on a dry land cotton farm.

Turner family a few years before Cecil was born. 1915. Back: Hubert, Coney, Newt Turner, Auti, mother-Emma Pearl McClain Turner, Irene. Front: Ava, Cassie, baby Veltie.

School photo in 1920's at Roscoe, Texas. Cecil Turner kneels on the front row far right.

His parents named him Cecil Edwin Turner at birth and welcomed him into a large farming family near Roscoe, Texas. The Turner clan had been there for many years. The historical marker at the Roscoe Cemetery records how my great grandfather donated the land for the site, and buried a relative in the first grave. However, the Turner heritage was not one of wealth, but one of hard work and love of the land and God. Even at a young age, my father had a strong love of God and the local church. I recall a story he disclosed of a family prayer meeting. He felt God's presence with such an overwhelming power, he went outside to weep before his Lord. This sounded strange to my little Baptist ears and I am sure it was not a common occurrence in his family or church. However, I have thought back to this story several times over the years. It seemed God had his hand on my dad at an early age.

My father was very proud of his military service. He did not speak of it often, but when he did, you could tell it was an important part of his life. I remember stopping by to visit a few army buddies when we were on vacation and heard them talk about "whatever happened to ole' so and so—remember when he almost got us all killed?" Dad kept in touch with some of those men for years. I knew he was proud to be a veteran and had dreamed of going back to Europe to see the places he had fought for and occupied as a young man. He told us a few stories of life in the service—getting leave from boot camp to attend his mother's funeral, the friendly European people, and about his job as radio operator. We had seen a few photos of army jeeps and far off places and people. Dad wisely waited until I was an adult before he showed me the gruesome photos of the concentration camps he helped liberate. I did not know, however, that he received a commendation for bravery or that his term of service spanned the entirety of our involvement in World War II. The more letters I read, the more it seemed that *his* war story painted in faithful letters was *our* war story.

I cannot imagine how he found time to write so many letters, but I am perhaps as grateful as his anxious family he was so faithful to write. It is an absolute miracle the letters survived so well over the years. Someone recognized the importance of the letters and carefully protected them in the homemade album. Alzheimer's disease ravaged my mother's memory and she could shed no light on the mystery. Perhaps my father's stepmother kept and arranged the letters for her new stepson. Just keeping up with 154 letters and all the photographs was no small task. I suspect, however, my mother probably built and assembled the album to protect these precious letters. She made scrapbooks of her own early mementos so I can envision her assembling the book for her new husband. Mother had returned to Sweetwater, Texas after years of nurse's training in Tennessee during the war. She came very close to marrying a young pilot she met but returned home after the war claimed his life. In the letters, you will read how my father considered the possibility of a war bride, but in the end came home and fell in love with a local nurse.

My father, as his father before him, had a deep abiding faith in God. It is a legacy, thankfully, that has continued through two more generations. I wish I could say the same for our nation. In today's climate of political correctness, some might expect to see an apology for the beliefs expressed in these letters. None will be given. These chapters contain each sentence exactly as the words flowed from the homesick heart of a young Christian who, like our nation, endured a test to the very core of his foundation. Perhaps this is not a big story, but as I read these treasures in letters and photos, I felt they were not just about my father. Four historic years of our nation's life lay woven within the lines of correspondence and compelled me to share them with more than just family. For those of you that have lived similar stories, perhaps they will bring back those tragic yet heroic days. For those of us that have only heard about those hard times, perhaps the letters of Cecil Turner will make them come alive.

CHAPTER 1

★ ★ ★ ★ ★

Training Camps

*When I was a child, I spoke as a child, I understood
as a child, I thought as a child; but when I became
a man, I put away childish things.*

I Corinthians 13: 11 (NKJV)

A large statue dominates the west entrance to the Texas State Capitol Building in honor of the predominately Texas division distinguished in two wars. Many Texans proudly recall the "T Patch" Division that fought courageously in World War II. The 36th Division adopted their defining insignia in 1918. The easily distinguished patch consisted of an olive drab 'T' on a blue flint arrowhead. Newly organized units from the National Guard of Oklahoma and Texas comprised the 36th in World War I. The blue arrowhead represents the State of Oklahoma (once the Indian Territory), and the "T" is for Texas. Following World War I, the Army dissolved and reorganized the 36th under the Texas National Guard. The division heard the mobilization call again when another war in Europe started heating up. On November 15, 1940, the Army of the United States of America welcomed the 36th Division once again into their ranks. The unit gathered several nicknames including "Panther," "Lone Star," "Texas" and "T-Patch" Division. Originally composed solely of Texas National Guardsmen, many Selective Service trainees later joined them at Camp Bowie, Texas to fill the Division to combat strength. Later on in the war, as casualties thinned their numbers, reinforcements came from all over the nation and gave it an a All-American flavor. The citizens of Texas, however, always considered it their own.

In 1937, three years before the Texas Division was reactivated, Cecil Turner graduated from high school and never gave a thought to joining the armed services. With very little knowledge of any branch of the military, events in Europe had little to do with the young graduate's farm life. One of the first in the family to receive a high school diploma, Turner planned to continue farming with his aging father. Three years later, however, Cecil and his two brothers, Veltie and Hubert, decided to invest in a grocery store at nearby Merkel, Texas. Veltie stayed on the farm, but Hubert and Cecil moved to Merkel to run the store. Cecil lost the toss of the coin and became the reluctant butcher. These brothers started a new life, unaware that events on the other side of the world would be affecting them before Turner's Grocery and Market celebrated its first anniversary.

Veltie Turner and younger brother, Cecil (right)

Hubert Turner in front of the Turner Grocery Store in early 1940's.

On March 7, 1941, twenty-three year old Cecil Turner took off his butcher apron and donned fatigues as he obeyed his draft notice. Hubert was left to run the store alone when his brother joined the 36th Division at Camp Bowie, located at Brownwood in Central Texas. Army life must have seemed strange indeed to a "Plowboy" from Roscoe. Those first few months were difficult, as it was for any new recruit. A crisis at home made the adjustment even more difficult. Cecil had just settled in when the Army gave him an emergency leave to attend his mother's funeral. None of his letters were saved during this time period, but it must have been painful—to receive the news from a stranger, travel back home alone, say a final good-bye to his mother, and leave his grieving father. His faith and relationship with God pulled him through this difficult period. During the next year, Cecil wrestled with wanting to be home helping his father and the need to keep his country safe from aggressors.

Jacob Newton Turner and Emma Pearl McClain Turner (circa 1940)

New recruit, Private Cecil Turner, wearing "Artillery Brass"

At his initial training at Camp Bowie, Cecil discovered and developed his skill as a radio operator. The Army used this expertise and assigned him to the Headquarters Battery of the 36th Division for most of his term in the military. As a radio operator, he learned to use code and terminology to transmit positions of enemy and friendly forces and coordinate the use of artillery. Letters from Cecil during this period were not saved, but many photographs were kept of his training camp months.

Father and son pose in their Army uniforms

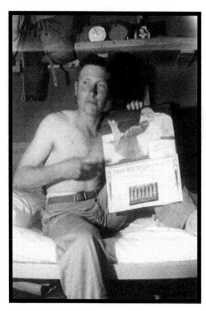

Cecil poses with the Turner Bros. Grocery & Market
calendar sent from brother, Hubert.

After a year in Texas, the 36th traveled to the swamplands of Louisiana to conduct a mock battle with the Third Army during September 1941. Later that fall, the Texans returned to their home base at Camp Bowie. Cecil was in Roscoe on a weekend leave when the unthinkable happened—"the day that will live in infamy." The December 7th news of Pearl Harbor struck fear and anger throughout the nation. Soldiers listening to the broadcast knew they would soon be called to stop America's new enemy. Cecil's brother-in-law, Howard Boston, was also in the service. He would soon be deployed to the Pacific front, leaving his wife, Ava, and their newborn son, little Howard. An uncertain future darkly emerged.

Wearing coverall style fatigues complete with hat, Cecil stands by a command car while going through maneuvers.

Boot camp days in Texas --taking a raw recruit and molding a soldier.

With the United States officially in the war, all training shifted into a more serious mode. The Texans moved overland to sandy Camp Blanding, Florida in February 1942. The commanders primed the group for early overseas shipment. However, the tenacity of the Texans was so impressive during the Florida maneuvers, the orders changed and so did the Division, as units departed and new recruits were added. The T-Patchers stayed in the states another year, training for a key invasion of Europe.

Wearing souvenir from Louisiana maneuvers

Guard duty--Cecil on the right, in WWI style Army helmet
carrying the M1903

Cecil is wearing the new 1 lb. helmet which the Army adopted in 1941.

All dressed up at Camp Blanding, Florida

Jacob Newton Turner, 1942

Life in Texas carried on while Cecil and many other sons practiced for war. Within a year, Hubert had left the grocery business and moved his family back to Roscoe to help his lonely father farm. Cecil received many letters from home while in training, but only two from his father, Newt, were saved. Newton Jacob Turner was born to a simple clan in Walker County, Georgia in 1877. He was the oldest son of a large family that moved to Nolan County, Texas when he was seven-years-old. In those days, farming sons were needed at home; thus few ever finished school. With limited formal education, however, Newt farmed successfully and read his beloved Bible. Love for Cecil compelled the self-conscious father to put his thoughts on paper as best he could in spite of limited literacy.

Roscoe, Tex March 11

My Dear son Cecil I got your letters and cards so glad to get them I am all right had a good rain and will be busy planting now Veltie is better think he will get all right. hope you will get to come home to see me soon.

Son sometimes I get lonesome and blue and I cry unto my Lord and he puts his everlasting arm beneath me and let me see the Heavenly so praise his name.

Wheat is looking good now Hubert is building a new home son you was received in the church last Sunday. son all the kids is so good to me. And all the Church here is so good to me. Grany is getting mity weak. If you can get a furlo and fly home I will be glad to furnesh the money Son you no I can't right no good. But you are on my mind and in my prayer all time.

Dad

On the back of the picture of his new home, Hubert writes,"Gee I would like a long letter from you, did you ever write Maxie? (Hubert's Daughter, Cecil's niece) Is hot and dry here, cotton will make about 1/4 bale, would like to be in the grocery business again. Think of you much, your Bro. HLT"

Enjoying the Florida beaches

While in Florida, Cecil visited historical St. Augustine. Impressed by this beautiful old city, he vowed to bring his bride there someday for their honeymoon. No letters were saved to document his stay in Florida, but several photos from the beach indicate his stay was not all bad.

In front of the Hotel Ponce Deleon in San Augustine, Florida, where Turner vowed to take his bride one day.

From: N. J. Turner
Pvt. Cecil Turner
Headquarters Battery
36th Division Artillery
Roscoe, Tex.
Monday 2

Dear son I recived your letters and cards and was so glad to hear from you. It is cold here, some rain and snow Sunday. I am alone but the Lord is with me. I am doing fine. I got a letter from Ava and Joyce this morning they are OK. Gran is looking good. Son I wish I could be at your side to get them Japs. Son don't weary about me I will get along all right.

may the love of God be with you is my prayer

dad

After extensive maneuvers in the warm Carolinas during July and August of 1942, the 36th moved north to a station on Cape Cod at Camp Edwards, Massachusetts. Living in tent cities, Cecil's Division practiced the new art of amphibious operations and launched a mock invasion of Martha's Vineyard in late October. Boston and area villages enjoyed their "Texans," as they called them, and followed their advances in the war effort. Cecil had several entries in his address book of local girls and families he met. The blustery winter on the Cape in 1942 cold-tested the 36th Division at twenty degrees below zero.

Boston welcomed the troops.

Dressed and ready to see Cape Cod (Cecil on the left)

Touring the Massachusetts area history.

The 36th was trained and ready as an overseas departure loomed closer every day. The Division spread out furloughs for the men at the close of 1942 to ready them for quick deployment. On a short Texas visit, Cecil became acquainted with his father's new wife, Martha. Newt Turner had not enjoyed the lonely life of a widower and married a Roscoe widow to fill the void. The friendly visit produced two favorable effects: Cecil referred to her as "Mom" in the remainder of the letters and Martha began saving letters from her stepson for the remainder of the war.

Cecil's new stepmother, Martha, writes, "This was made at a friend's at Sweetwater. A short time before I was your Mom."

Martha and Newt Turner in early 1943.

Camp Edwards
Nov. 11, 1942

Dear Mom and Dad,

I should have written on the way or at least as soon as I got here but I just didn't. This is the end of the first day of duty. This morning we had a hike and I thought it would be a little rough so soon after a furlough but it didn't bother me at all!

We rolled into Boston at noon Tuesday alright. That's as good as any of the boys have done. I am glad I took my furlough when I did. Anything could happen and I have mine already over.

Boy! The news is still coming in good. I just hope the French cooperate and the Lord being willing we will 'mow em' down.'

I'll write again soon. I don't seem to be in the right mood to write tonight.

We are in warm barracks, too warm almost.

It was nice of you to offer to fix the chicken, Mom, but the fellow who met me in Forth Worth had a box of chicken and we still had some left when we got to Boston.

There were so few young people at Roscoe—no one of the "old class." Then what do you suppose happened. I was about to eat supper in the diner and Lucy Ellen Gathing and Pauline Calhoun called me across the isle.—it was nice to see some Roscoe people. They were going to see Emma Gathing who is married and living in N.Y.

We have been requested to listen to a message tonite at 10:30 so I'll say Bye now.

Lovingly,
Cecil

The Texans had been training for over two years with still no indication of when and where they would join the war. Early in 1943, elements of the 36th Division traveled to a military reservation in Virginia for training in combat on mountainous terrain—invaluable experience for the battles to come.

The photo reads, "17 below zero"

Camp Edwards, Mass.
March 9, 1943

Dear Folks,

I'm still O.K.

I'm not hearing from anyone, got one letter from Veltie.
Would like to hear from all at least once.

My mail may not be getting through to me.

All my love
Cecil

Don't forget to use V-mail when you write Howard.

I am going to have $40 sent home from Wash. to you each
month Dad and you can put it in the bank for me.
L.
C.T.

The war department developed a high tech answer to the problem of the magnitude of mail delivered between the servicemen and home. V-Mail letters were written on forms that families could purchase at five and ten cent stores or the post office. These special forms were photographed, put on film, flown across the world and then reproduced at the mail center closest to the soldier's position. The quality might be inferior but Uncle Sam promised faster delivery to those who would use the one-sided sheet. The V-Mail system reduced the time it took a soldier to receive a letter by a month—from six weeks by boat to twelve days or less by air. The same was true for the V-Mail forms provided for soldiers to send letters home. However, the main advantage of V-Mail was its compact nature. Reduction in the size and weight of the letters translated into more space for crucial military supplies on cargo planes. One advertisement explained that 1,700 V-Mail letters could fit in a cigarette packet, while reducing the weight of the letters in paper form by 98%. Transport of the letters by plane minimized the chances that the enemy would intercept the letters, although writers were reminded to delete any information that might prove useful to the enemy in case some V-Mail was captured.

Cecil knew he needed divine intervention in order to make it home from the war. He also worried about his family. Losing one parent made him anxious concerning his father's health and he prayed God's blessing on them. His plea for prayers demonstrated faith in his family's prayer life and to the God they prayed. James 4:2 tells us, "you do not have because you do not ask" (NKJV). Cecil was one to take advantage of the power of prayer. Forty years later, he would record in his journal, "Whatever God wants to do here on earth, He made prayer the key to it!"

Camp Edwards, Mass.
March 19, 1943

Dearest Dad and Mom,

I'm feeling fine tonite. I hope both of you are well.

I have been very busy lately. We finished our explosive work. You know I said we were through with it when I was at home but when I got back we had a full week more. We gave all the fellows the exercise this time without a single man getting hurt. We're through now.

We'll be leaving for parts unknown but I don't know when or where. Don't ask any questions in your letter but I would like to hear from home again. I got your letter written on the 14th.

May God bless you and let me leave this thought—I want you, Dad, to always take care of yourself. You always had a tendency to work too hard. I wish I could be at home to take your plow like I used to work with you. But everything always works out for the best. Mom, I know you will always take care of yourself. You seem to have learned to do that long ago. I know you are convincing Dad that he should quit work.

Always remember me when you talk to the Lord and I'll be coming home some day.

All my love,
Cecil

Tell them all hello. Remember V-Mail.

Cecil's sister, Ava, and nephew, H.C. Boston Jr.

Mar. 30, '43
Camp Edward, Mass.

Dear Dad & Mom,

How are you? Huh?

Guess I can't hear you–Wish I could.

I'm sending this $40 money order. If you will put it in the bank for me I will appreciate it. The $40 allotment will start next month.
Heard from Veltie & Ava yesterday. I am fine but in a hurry.

God Bless You,

Love,
Cecil

Within three days, Cecil boarded a ship leaving the New York Port of Embarkation with the rest of the 36th Division bound for Oran, Algeria. A fast convoy of ships made the trip in just 11 days.

CHAPTER 2

★ ★ ★ ★ ★

North Africa

*I thank my God upon every remembrance of you,
always in every prayer of mine making request for
you all with joy*

Philippians 1:3 (NKJV)

Ship newsletter on the troop carrier, April 1943.

Trick played on rookies during shipment to North Africa

Spring flowers and green valleys surprised T-Patchers in North Africa. They quickly proceeded 100 miles inland to a training ground at Magenta. Until Rommel's Afrika Corps was decisively whipped at Tunis and Bizerte, the 36th Division was held in combat reserve.

Cecil gets a different ride during a stopped convoy to
Magenta, North Africa.

April 15, 1943

Dearest Dad & Mom,

Here I am in North Africa and feeling fine. The trip over was like a pleasure trip. Things are much better than I expected.

I wish you would let all of the folks read this as I may not get to write everyday. Tell Veltie that I saw T-Bone and he is fine and healthy. I could mention Hubert's, Auti's, Coney's, Cassie's, Ava's, and Irene's family by name but I won't. I think of everybody a lot. I would like to see Veltie and Doris and my little name-sake. How is he? Tell Hubert to go ahead and buy me a heifer. Ha! If you see Joyce Elrod tell her I wish she were here to help me with my French. I didn't hear from Joyce the last few days I was in the USA. Guess she is still in Cal. Tell her I want her to go to Church every Sunday and ask the Lord to let us win if we deserve it and it is His will. Wish I could see her. There are a lot of things I will have to talk about. I have seen interesting things here in this old country. Dad, we are not the only people who can grow wheat. Dad, I think of you and mom a lot and want you to always remember me when you pray. Ask the Lord to bring me back to the ones I love. Give us the courage to overcome the enemy.

I love you,
Cecil

Family is never more important than when they are far away. Cecil was part of a large, close family who formed his support and lifeline. Hubert, Auti, and Velti were brothers with growing families. Veltie, closest in age to Cecil, had been crippled by polio in his youth. He and wife, Doris, named their first son after Cecil—Ronald *Edwin* Turner.

Irene, Cassie, Coney, and Ava were older, married sisters. Joyce was the baby of the family—the only sibling younger than Cecil. The love, support, and prayers of his family kept Cecil grounded in the truths that guided his life. Other hometown folks and family were mentioned frequently in his letters. Joyce Elrod was his pastor's daughter and longtime friend. Cecil's cousin, Roberta (Bert), was also faithful to write while he was overseas.

Ronald Edwin Turner (held by mother, Doris) was named for his uncle, Cecil Edwin, while away at war.

Cecil's sister, Joyce, in San Diego

Luke 10:19 speaks of having the courage and power to be victorious over the enemy. This was Cecil's prayer: triumph "over all the power of the enemy: and nothing shall by any means hurt you." He saw his father on his knees many times and knew there was power from that posture. Evidence of the Holy Spirit in his father's life gave him confidence in his father's prayers. Years later, Cecil wrote in a spiritual journal, "The source of power of the Christian is the inwardly real presence of the Holy Spirit of God."

Nicknames are common in the military and it did not take long for Cecil to be dubbed, "Deacon." Perhaps it was unusual for a young man to live what he believed in front of his peers, especially in a time of war. There may have been some ridicule for his clean language, moral behavior, and faithful church attendance, but none was ever mentioned. It is more likely that a respect was earned after months of consistently living his faith out in front of his Battery.

April 25, 1943

Dear Dad & Mom,

I should go to bed but let me write this letter first. I am a little sleepy being Corporal of the guard last nite and today. Today was the first time I ever went to Church armed. Being Corporal of the guard I took my gun along but was not disturbed at all during the Service. In case of fire or disorder I was supposed to be ready. It made me think of the Pilgrims. It rained a little and we didn't have such a big crowd at Easter Service. We had a Good Friday Service the other day and observed the Lord's Supper. The Chaplain asked four of us to serve the trays of wine and bread. Wish both of you could have experienced that outdoor Service.

There was never a moon so pretty in Texas as the one I saw the night of the 22nd. More like a spotlight.

Nearly all of the boys are getting mail now but I have not received any yet—maybe soon. I thought of home more today than usual. I am fine and healthy. Wish you would tell everybody hello for me. I think of my Dad and Mom a lot and all the family.

Write me,
All my love,
Cecil

Not like the sparrows in Roscoe

Corporal Cecil Turner

H. L. Westbrook
Route III
Roscoe, Texas
U.S.A.

Pfc. Cecil Turner
[Sender's name]
Hq 36th Div. Art-Apo
[Sender's address]
Apo P.M. New York City

4/28/43
[Date]

Dear Coney, Herman, Kiddies, Cassie, Dinky, & all,

Greetings from north Africa and from a guy who thinks of you a whale of a lot. Maybe africa should never have been called the Dark Continent. I find it nice here and I wish you could see the wild flowers. I never saw so many in Texas. I am fine and eating too much as usual. I wish all of you could attend one of our Services on Sunday. If some of you see Dora Dean Stevens you can tell her that I saw Albert Knight and he was doing fine. We had a long talk. They were married you know 'bout a year ago.

I hope I can send some pictures home of a few things I have seen. The Arabs are an interesting race of people. None of you have ever seen a moon in Texas that will compare with ours - more like a spotlight. Has Hubert got me a heifer calf yet? I must have a start. Ha. We have records and I hear N.B.C. program.

Always remember me in your prayers and the Lord being willing I will see you and take up life again.

Hello Dad & Mom!

All my love,
Cecil.

V - MAIL

April 28, 1943

Dear Coney, Herman, Kiddies, Cassie, Dinky, Ava & all,

Greetings from North Africa and from a guy who thinks of you a whole of a lot. Maybe Africa should never have been called the Dark Continent. I find it nice here and I wish you could see the wild flowers. I never saw so many in Texas. I am fine and eating too much as usual. I wish all of you could attend one of our Services on Sunday. If some of you see Dora Dean Stevens you can tell her that I saw Albert Knight and he was doing fine. We had a long talk. They were married you know about a year ago.

I hope I can send some pictures home of a few things I have seen. The Arabs are an interesting race of people. None of you have ever seen a moon in Texas that will compare with ours–more like a spotlight. Has Hubert got me a heifer calf yet? I must have a start. Ha!

We have records and I hear N.B.C. programs.

Always remember me in your prayers and the Lord being willing I will see you and take up a life again.

Hello Dad & Mom!
All my love,
Cecil

Cecil (on top) with his buddies at the artillery park of a heavy artillery battery.
The 155 mm "Schneiders" were modeled and a WWI French design.

Cecil feels the miles from home, especially at night.

Deacon Turner was faithful to pray and ask for prayer with I John 5:14 in mind: "Now this is the confidence that we have in him, that if we ask any thing according to his will, he hears us" (NKJV).

Most of the letters seemed to have three main purposes: to let his family know he was safe, to ask them to pray, and to make sure they knew how much he loved them.

It was a difficult task to discuss serious matters without worrying his family. Rarely did Cecil relay any message which would cause them to worry. On the contrary, he must have felt it was his duty to not cause any more stress on his aging father. Between this concern and the restrictions on discussing any military specifics, we must repeatedly guess what new dangers dominated his thoughts and narrow escapes he endured.

May 5, 1943

Dearest Mom and Dad, YOUR FIRST LETTER CAME TODAY

I got your first letter today (one paragraph)

Here I am this pretty Thurs. morning and feeling fine except that I would like some mail. I am still a radio operator and like it pretty good. I am trying to learn all I can about electricity too but we don't have a lot of time for that. That might be worth something to us someday. Does Ava have a car yet? She hear from Howard? Let me know how many of my letters and papers you get. I sent a little ship's paper home. You might keep my letters for a scrap book for me. Dad, you should get your birth certificate and have it with the insurance papers. It will have to be sent in with an insurance claim to establish your age if you ever have to collect my insurance. Of course you won't tho.'

It would be nice to get little packages from home — Kodak film, 127 or 120, Roscoe Times, fountain pens, hard candy, etc. How is Granny & Irene? Everybody write!

Love to Dad and Mom
Cecil

May 10, 1943 North Africa

Dearest Dad,

I'll make this little note to you this time just to let you know your youngest little boy is thinking of you. Maybe if I make it to you alone you will write me yourself. Mom has been very good to write me for both of you.

Someday I hope to be able to tell you what it means to hear from home when you are so far from home.

Another reason for writing is to send this picture I made in the states.

I am fine and healthy and went to Mother's Day service yesterday.

Mom, you would give plenty to have these wild flowers in your yard.

Say hello to Ava & H.C. — I heard from Howard.
All my love,
Cecil

Evidently, Newt Turner had a close relationship with all his children. They all seemed very diligent to check on him and gathered with him for holidays. However, losing his wife so close to the time Cecil left for war perhaps formed a special bond between them, one that grew with the miles and years. He was very self-conscious about his weakness with a pen, but Martha was very good to write her stepson, perhaps with the encouragement of Newt. Cecil certainly missed the hours on the farm with his dad most of all and tried to fill that void with occasional letters just to him.

After several months in Magenta Valley, part of the 36th Division moved to secure a threatened area. In a political move to avert Spanish or German designs on French Morocco, two units—Division Headquarters and Special Troops—shuttled westward 500 miles to spend a leisurely summer in the cork forests near Rabat and Casablanca. As a radio operator with Division Headquarters for most of his tour, Deacon Turner spent much of his African training among these strange cork trees.

Radio operator Cecil leans on a smooth cork tree where the bark has been stripped.

Showing the folks at home their tent city among the
North African cork trees.

May 24, 1943

Dearest Mom, Dad, and all,

*Now I know you have heard from me. It was swell to get
your four letters today and a graduation announcement
from Betty Jo. I need to write you, Coney, Veltie, Ava
& Cassie. It's late and I can't write everybody. We have
traveled four days but are now settled down again. I am
going to send home a few things as soon as I get time. I
will send a roll of film home soon. They will come already
developed and will you (Veltie) send all the ones, not of
me, to the wife of my friend—Mrs. M. P. Kopanski, 2539
North Luna St., Chicago, Ill.—with a simple explanation.
He doesn't have a camera. I hope some of them are good.
By the way, I hope to get some little packages of 127 or
120 film (etc).*

My dear grandmother was a wonderful person and now she has passed on to her reward. I was expecting to hear of her death and I am almost ashamed that I didn't mourn her death with all of you. I can hardly realize she is gone.

Saw an Int. combine today and F-12 Farmall.–Wheat growing on a hill I could hardly climb.

I would like to see you. Hi Dad!
Love,
Cecil

Many changes had occurred in the Turner family since Cecil took off his farm clothes to wear his army uniform. All soldiers experienced losses during the war, but not many lost their mother and grandmother. Letters to and from home helped the mourning process and eased the ache of missing his grandmother's funeral.

One of the best ways Deacon Turner escaped a situation was to play back memories of better days and folks at home. Every train whistle took Cecil back to the tracks that carried the Roscoe, Snyder and Pacific Railroad (R. S. and P.) near his home. Life at Roscoe was so predictable that it brought comfort to picture familiar scenes and summer revival meetings. Even after two years in the military, Cecil was never far from the farm boy who missed the land, the crops and the people that worked them.

June 1, 1943

Dearest Mom and Dad,

It's about time I should tell you that I am going along fine in every respect. I went to town last week and bought some things to send home when I get time Memorial Day. I was in a guard of honor in a ceremony in honor of Americans and French servicemen who were buried at the same cemetery.

I think of you often and try to imagine what is going on at home. Some of the farmers who weren't so good at farming I guess are planting some June cotton. The corn is as green as poison, maybe. The harvest may be in full swing unless wheat is not very early. I wonder if you got those old trucks to running.

You should see the cars and trucks here that burn charcoal. I saw a '36 Chevy. going down the road looking like the R. S. & P.

The summer meeting will be starting in a few weeks after you get this letter. I got a letter from Joy (Houston) in 11 days. Every time you write, tell Joyce I think of her lots.

God's blessing to you,
Cecil

His younger sister, Joyce, literally grew up while Cecil was overseas. They played through childhood days and survived the teenage years together. Now, an independent Joyce was going out on her own, with Cecil no longer able to give her big brother advice.

Bro. G. A. Elrod pastored the Roscoe Baptist Church for several years before World War II and throughout the conflict as well. Even on the other side of the world, Cecil valued his relationship with this Godly man and the church. He began to realize he had taken for granted many aspects of growing up in a Christian home where the church was an extension of his family.

June 6, 1943
Rev. G. A. Elrod

Dear Pastor,

I thought you might like to hear from one of your sheep even though I am one of your "black sheep." We had a short service this morning conducted by a Methodist Chaplain. The singing was good. We used a little field organ that is about three feet tall.

I'm wondering if the Brotherhood is active now. I know these must be trying times for all church activities but I sure hope that the Brotherhood is well organized and carrying on, Bro. Elrod. I wish when you visit in the different homes you would tell the parents how thankful they should be for the Christian environment they have in their section of the country. A junior in one of our churches is better informed than an Intermediate in churches in the Northern States and other states where I visited. A child has more opportunities in our churches.

If you know the addresses of any of our missionaries and they are in North Africa, I might get to contact them. The Summer Revival will soon begin no doubt. The Lord be with you in every good thing you attempt. Say hello to all your family. I hope they are well. Remember me when you speak to the Lord.

Always,
Cecil

In notes made while preparing for Sunday School over thirty years later, Cecil wrote this question, "Do you ask the pastor to pray for you because he has a better batting average?" His answer to the question concerning Bro. Elrod would probably be, "Yes!" He respected and admired his pastor after seeing him walk and talk God's Word before him. There were not many soldiers around him who had the church background Cecil enjoyed. That background anchored his mind and spirit through the lonely, dangerous, and difficult days ahead.

Mrs. H. C. Boston
June 6, 1943

My Dear Sister,

Your letter of May 21 came half and hour ago so I won't waste a minute in answering. I am glad to hear of your meeting and it sounds like you have a nice set up. So H. C. is a year old now, huh? I bet he is getting "cuter" every day.

I have heard several transcribed programs today from NBC broadcasts. It's fun even if they are quite late.

We had a pretty nice service yesterday. A Methodist Chaplain is in charge.

Say hello to everybody, Ava, and keep 'm on the bean.

No, I didn't feed the fish coming over. I wasn't sick at all. Some of the boys were very seasick but I wasn't. I rather enjoyed the trip. I was always out on deck for an hour or more at night just watching the sea.

If I have to leave several out of a box of gifts I send home, you help them understand. I can't find something for everybody.

There's not a whole lot to write. I'll write everything and every time I can.

Lots of love
Cecil

His sweet sister, Ava, was faithful to write during the entire war. She also must have been a Christian leader in her family and church as well, thus, the remark: "Keep 'm on the bean." Ava felt the sting of separation from her husband *and* brother due to the war and was sensitive to Cecil's need to hear from home, especially concerning their dad.

Newton Turner with daughter, Ava, and grandson H.C.

Dear Mom and Dad, June (10), 1943

I'll start this letter tonight and finish later. I'm listening to the American Expeditionary Station. A station created just to entertain us.

(24 hrs. later) The news came over the radio that Rep. Baldwin introduced a bill to give servicemen a 100 dollar

bonus after the war for every year of service. Maybe I will have a little bit more to help me get a start. I am going to send some money home from here too.

(Sunday 13ᵗʰ) Yesterday I was in town for the afternoon. I bought some more things to send home. I can't find a thing hardly for a girl or a woman.

Got a letter yesterday from Cassie and Dinky. I would like to know what is going on back in the States especially at home.

Be good and remember me
Love,
Cecil

While he was still in training and not involved in armed conflict, Cecil tried hard to send souvenirs from a foreign land. He wanted to include all his family and friends so they would know how much they meant to him. Trips to nearby towns were infrequent but Cecil had managed to gather several items that would indeed be foreign to his Texas loved ones.

June 18, 1943

Dear Mom and Dad, (Need a good combine man?)

I got your letter written on June 2, this morning and it was very nice hearing from home again. Already I appreciate the candy you are sending me even though it will be a few days yet before it arrives. I am going to sit up a little later tonite and start packing a box for you and part of the "Gang." There won't be something for everybody but tell them I will try to send more when I can. The nicest gift I will send to you, Mom, so that when the kids come by to see you they will see it and think of me.

I ripped a corner out of the tent when I read that Howard was coming home. Ava, I am so glad! I know he could hardly wait to see his little fellow. I wish I could have been there. I wonder where he is now.

I got a letter from Veltie, Cassie, and Joyce Elrod. I am wondering whether you got the little ship's paper or it may have been an African Service paper. I can't get over Howard being home. How nice!

Don't ever worry about me. I wouldn't be any safer if I was at home.

Hello to all,
Remember me always,
Cecil

The joy Cecil conveys at hearing of Howard's furlough was genuine. His sweet Ava would see her husband. Little H.C., Jr. could get to know his father and they could be a family for a while. It must have been hard, however, for Cecil to picture them all welcoming Howard home while he was still so far from them.

June 20, 1943

My dear Dad,North Africa, Africa

I didn't intend to write you today but after going to the services a while ago, I decided to tell you again how much I think of you and what a swell dad you have been to me.

The Chaplain mentioned Biblical examples of the relations of Father and Son. Now that you are getting up nearly the middle age mark, I want you to know that this boy thinks you have done a good job of raising a family. I want to do everything in my power to see that you live out the rest of your life in peace and comfort. Right now I am not able to contribute much but I know you understand that and sometimes I think you are actually proud of me over here in this remote part of the world even though I don't deserve it. I hope I get to wave at you from the gang-plank soon or meet you at the train station. Meanwhile, I'll keep a stiff upper lip, a high chin, and keep pluggin.'

I have a friend who never has seen his dad that he can remember. He deserted him when his mother died and he had to run away to keep from being sent to the orphans home. So you see I also know what it means to grow up without a dad. You are a swell dad!

Your kid,
Cecil

P.S. I hope you don't forget to raise the concave when you hit the weeds and put on the screens to keep out the trash. Does that little idler still get dry and growl? Ha!

P.S. no. 2, I am enclosing a cheap picture of myself and 2 ten franc notes. A ten franc note is equal to 20 cents in US money. Show them to the "Gang" when they come by.

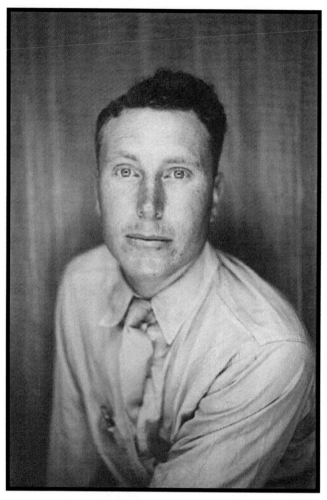

The "cheap" picture Cecil sent to his dad.

Even if Martha had not started keeping all the letters, surely Newt would have kept this sweet tribute. Theirs was a special relationship, cherished by both father and son. The hardest times to be away from home were holidays and birthdays. The war had separated Cecil from his dad for the third Father's Day in a row. Each time he tried to let his father know he was not forgotten.

Western Union Telegram
NJ Turner
MY LOVE AND GREETINGS ON FATHERS DAY
MY THOUGHTS ARE WITH YOU WELL
CECIL TURNER

105 pm June 25, 1943

The GI's had to be very careful in their letters home. There was always the possibility some information might inadvertently be included that could be used to discover the exact location of the Army. Every letter was reviewed by censors armed with black markers before it was put in the mail. Any information deemed risky would be blackened out from the letter. (XXXX)

June 24, 1943

Dearest Mom and Dad,

I got one of your letters today so I'll try and give a fast reply. The box I have talked so much about has been mailed. I hope everyone enjoys the little things. I will send another box soon. I got a real nice letter from Louise Patterson. She is back in Merkel for the summer now. You remember I went to Denton to see her. She is a junior next year. The hot weather is coming on now. Directly after lunch I checked the thermometer and it was XXX in the shade.

I got two letters from Veltie today also. He's good to write also and I'll never forget. The box you sent will probably be here soon. I can't wait for it. We are getting some candy here so you can eat all the candy you can buy. The other day I was in a grocery store and you should see the difference between ours and an African store. I managed to be friendly with the clerk and managed to spit out enough French to tell them I was an old grocer.

I am fine and weigh as much or more than ever. Hello to Ava, Cassie, & Coney. Haven't heard from Joyce!

Love,
Cecil

While on a trip to a town in Algeria, Cecil snaps a picture of the Army band playing for the residents.

Still training in North Africa

Mail call was always the highlight of every soldier's day. A letter could brighten even the darkest day and a package from home was like winning the lottery. Every item brought back sights and smells from home, and with few books and magazines in their tents, labels became nighttime reading material.

Dear Mom & Dad,   June 28, '43

The box arrived on the 26th two days ago. The candy was swell and I have finished one of the rolls of film already. I'll soon have them on the way home. I won't be giving much of the candy away. I know Dad bought the stick candy. That was always his favorite. I notice it was made in Fort Worth. That looked good too. The pen and the film are the nicest. I appreciate the package very much and I hope you in turn enjoy the one I sent. I don't know whether you could get the Sweetwater Reporter or Roscoe Times sent to me or not. I have just heard the news over the radio and all of it was good. There is a good program of American music on now.

I got a letter from Aunt Iva and it seemed they were doing unusually good. Maybe I told you I finally heard from Joyce and she sent me a good picture of her and her roommate.

Love,
Cecil

Sister Joyce with roommate in California

At times it seemed as though Cecil was preoccupied with money—getting it, saving it, making sure it was going home. Perhaps it was just a reflection of the focus he was trying to maintain during the years he served in the military. Everyday his mind would think over the plans for his return to Texas. His heart's desire was to be back on the farm. By saving his military pay, he would be able to buy equipment and live his dream. The Bible tells us, "For where your treasure is, there your heart will be also" (Matthew 6:21, NKJV). Since Cecil's heart was still in Roscoe, it only made sense that his treasure should go there also.

July 1, 1943

Dear Mom & Dad,   North Africa, "Africa"

After getting paid yesterday I got a $50 money order and I'll enclose it. Put it in the bank for me when you have time. I had better save if I can—might need it some day. I hope you have been getting all of my letters. I've written pretty often. There's not a thing to write so be good and tell everybody hello.

Love,
Cecil

Let me know when you get this money order so I can throw away my receipt.

People who have never farmed or been around farming may have trouble identifying with Cecil's continued interest in crops at home and abroad. It is an occupation and way of life that is difficult to replace satisfactorily. Although George Washington gave most of his life to public service, his greatest desire was to return to his farm in Virginia. He stated that farming as an occupation "may be more conducive than almost any other to the happiness of mankind." [1]

Dearest Mom & Dad,
"4" JULY '43

Yesterday I received the best letter I have ever gotten from you because both of you wrote it. Now I know what was happening on June 20 at home. That was only two weeks ago. The wheat was good this year evidently. Did you sell and what is wheat worth? I hope I can send a sample *or bring back myself a pound or two of North African wheat. Some grains are twice as large as ours and one head will shell a handful. Maybe we would try a path in the garden. This being July 4, the chaplain spoke mainly on the subject of "Patriotic Christians." Mom, I'm sorry to hear that Theresa is bothered with arthritis. We should all be thankful for health and try to help those who aren't so fortunate. I sent a $50 money order home that may have gotten there by now or will in a few days. So Bobby Wash wanted my address. Well she can get it from someone. Both of you don't work too hard and, Mom, you see that Dad writes everytime if he isn't too busy. I got another letter from Cassie and one from Mae Wheeler.*

Hello to all!
Love always,
Cecil

The 36th Division formed the backbone of the newly organized 5th Army. Some of these troops took part in the Army's Invasion Training Center at Arzew, on the Mediterranean. Even though the 36th had not seen combat, they were called on to take the 1st and 45th Divisions through the paces before these men were shipped to the Sicily invasion. While working at this Training Center, Cecil developed and sharpened a new skill—French. This tool would become even more valuable in the days ahead.

July 11, '43

Dearest Mom and Dad,

I have been pretty busy the last few days. Since I last wrote I have had the day off. I went to church this morning and heard a new Chaplain from another division. I should be back with my old Hq. in about 20 days.

How is everything at home? I am fine in every way. You should see me now—the first Turner with real brown skin. This African sun has given me a good tan. I'll be glad when I get my mail again and that should be soon. I don't think I have ever gotten a letter from Hubert. Maybe they got lost or maybe they are on the way now. My French is getting better now. I can say anything I want to now but it sounds funny to them. I hope both of you are feeling well. Always remember me when you pray.

> *Love always,*
> *Cecil*

Looking more tan after months in Africa.

July 18, '43

Dearest Mom & Dad,

Another week has passed and I am still doing fine. I am still at the 5th Army Leadership and Battle Training Center.

I sure would have liked being at church this morning back at home. I never get homesick or blue but sometimes I get the ole' wish I was home feeling. Ask Veltie if R.E. Broadwell is home yet and how he is doing. Tell him hello. I heard he was home now. I am with a group of fellows from close around home — Loraine, Snyder, Santa Anna, Merkel, etc. Tell Hubert I ran into an officer who left Merkel in 1936 and he and I used to go with Vivian Davis. I was surprised when he pulled out her picture. I guess Howard is back on duty now. I bet Ava and little H.C. enjoyed his stay. Tell everyone I will try to write more in about ten days. I hope both of you are fine. Always remember me in your prayers.

Love,
Cecil

Cecil with the 36th Division in North Africa

Cecil points himself out in a picture with buddies relaxing on a beach at Port Lyautey, French Morocco, North Africa.

The *Baptist Standard* is a weekly newspaper which Texas Baptists have been reading for many generations. It chronicles church events all over the state as well as articles written by preachers and laymen. Cecil had grown up with copies of the *Baptist Standard* around the house. The periodical was one more link to home, his church, and his faith.

August 8, '43

Dearest Mom & Dad,

I received your letter written on July 14ᵗʰ and I was glad to hear that you had gotten the box I sent home. I sincerely hope you do enjoy the things I sent.

I am doing fine—never felt fitter.

Surely it must have been hard for Howard to leave but he may be lucky and stay in the States now. Wish I could have seen him.

I went to two Services this morning conducted by the Chaplain. The Baptist Standard comes to us pretty often and I read of the happenings in Texas. I got a letter from Mozelle Dement the other day. Also letters from Hubert, Auti, Buster, Duncan, etc.

I wish you could see hundreds of acres of ripe grapes that they have here in Africa. Did any of the pictures show up that I sent home to Veltie?

It should be easier for me to write more often now so I will try.

All of my love and don't forget me when you pray.

Love,
Cecil

Cecil constantly reminded his family to continue interceding on his behalf for safety and victory. Prayer became a priority in Cecil's life that continued to increase throughout the years. Perhaps it can be traced to this time when he desperately needed them to remember him when they prayed. Years later as an avid prayer warrior, he wrote in his journal, "God forbid that I should sin against the Lord in ceasing to pray for you"

(I Samuel 12:23, KJV).

20 Aug 43

Dearest Mom & Dad,

Another letter came today so I will answer right back. I have been getting a nice bit of mail lately. Cassie writes pretty often. Yes, I did get the package you sent and I have mentioned getting it more than once in my letter. Some of my letters must not get through. The candy was delicious, the pen useful, and the film. I was and am still proud of it. Evidently the roll of film that I mailed home hasn't gotten there yet. I sent it to Veltie. I'll send more.

Things must be looking pretty good now at home. No limit on cotton and wheat, that should be alright.——This is Sunday the next day and I just returned from a short service we had here in our battery. I'm sure getting old–25 yrs. The other day, Aug. 13. Even if I am 30 when I get back I intend to start over at 21 and be a kid again. Do the $40 checks come each month from Wash? I'm glad the $50 money order arrived from me. I appreciate you writing me often–it is so nice to hear from home.

You mentioned sending me things. There's not a whole lot that you could send me that I need. Send me a few pictures (air mail) sometime, maybe some peanut candy. The natives are busy gathering grapes by the wagon load. Remember me to everybody.

Love,
Cecil

    This was Cecil's third birthday away from home and the training continued. In his letters, he expressed a subtle and sometimes not so subtle desire to return to the life he left —- even with all the changes at home.

Somewhere in North Africa

August 31, 1943

Dearest Dad & Mom,

This Tuesday afternoon finds me OK. I am sending another $50 money order for you to deposit for me if you please. If I get back, and I know I will, I'll have a little money.

Dad, I would write more long air-mail letters but there just isn't a thing to write about. We, like all other troops, are just waiting till the day when we see fit to defeat the Germans in Europe.

I get tired of writing home that I am getting plenty to eat, a good place to sleep, plenty of everything I need. Maybe that situation will change.

I'll bet things are sure booming in Texas now. Next year you will be planting all of the wheat and cotton you want. I sure would like to be there to walk over the farm with you and smoke a King Edward cigar with you. With you as the boss and me leading all the help, I believe we could handle a small country.

Mom, I guess most of your letters are getting through but I haven't received any mail for several days now. Maybe I am suffering for a 30 day period that I didn't write much. Tell everybody hello.

Love to you both,
Cecil

In a few short days, the 36th Division left the cork forests of North Africa, loaded on transport ships and headed toward the beaches of Salerno, Italy. For over two and a half years, Cecil and the T-Patchers had been training to become combat-ready for the invasion of Europe. During transport, each man could only hope and pray their training would get them through the danger that lay ahead of them.

As Cecil crossed the Mediterranean Sea, he must have prayed for the success of their mission, but his heart was also clinging to words from his father. In a letter that was lost, Newt revealed a promise from God. Cecil referred to this "promise letter" at the end of the war. While praying one day, Newt felt God clearly speak to him that his son would be coming home from the war. To read this in a father's letter would bring an emotional response from any son. To Cecil, however, it was more than just an encouraging message from home. He knew his father's prayer life was as strong as his relationship with the God they both loved. Newt trusted the truth of the message enough to tell his son. This must have given Cecil great hope. God *would* protect him and carry him through the dangerous days ahead and back home to his loved ones. The next two years would be a test of faith for both father and son as they clung to the promise in spite of circumstances. This would be a war not just against the evils of Nazism, but also doubts and fear. Later in his life, Cecil would quote many times the verse that states, "Perfect love casts out all fear" (I John 4:18, NKJV). Thirty years before on foreign soils, far from home, God's love had proved true to the young Christian.

Troops are getting ready for transport

Loaded and ready for European invasion.

Souvenir from the transport to the beaches of Salerno

CHAPTER 3

Italy

Therefore take up the whole armor of God, that
you may be able to withstand in the evil day

Ephesians 6:13 (NKJV)

Organized just two and a half years earlier, the new 36th Division had never seen combat. The Texans were poised to invade Italy in an operation named "Avalanche," the Allies' first amphibious landing on the European mainland. Cecil crossed the Mediterranean on the *U.S.S. Funston.* A post-war pamphlet detailed the action of the 36th.

In the pre-dawn blackness of September 9, 1943, T-Patchers tumbled off the [ladder] ropes into small landing craft bobbing on Salerno Bay. They were eager and ready for their first combat mission. The threat of invasion had forced Italy's surrender, and the announcement made just nine hours before the jump-off, had spread rapidly throughout the ships. Some men thought the invasion would be cancelled, but the operation went ahead.[1]

Confident, tough soldiers gazed ahead at the beach, assuming the landing would be a cinch, unaware that Italy's surrender did not mean Germany's withdrawal.

Salerno was a fierce baptism by fire for the 36th. The small landing boats bucked the surf until grounded on the shallow water of the beach. Men charged ashore, cutting paths through minefields and barbed wire. An enemy outpost marked them with machine gun tracers. Germans were waiting with artillery on the ridges and tanks on the flats.[2]

The landing had barely been accomplished when the Germans launched their first armored attack. On the right flank, Nazis barreled through to the beaches where a bloody man-to-tank action threw them back. On the left flank, two more armored spearheads slashed at the lines. One enemy assault nearly reached the 36th command post. In response, Allied artillery fire blasted the formation and destroyed five of thirteen tanks. The others fled. Americans had established their first post on European soil.[3]

Not every element of the invasion was successful. Some beachheads were impenetrable and the units were maneuvered laterally to follow behind those who had successfully landed. There were units split among the landing vessels, which caused some confusion in regrouping on the beaches. The Army would evaluate all aspects of the landing and apply the lessons in the Normandy invasion nine months later. A sad commentary in the evaluations praised the efficiency of one overworked group—the graves registration unit. However, the 36th Division, untried in battle, had landed under fire, overcome prepared beach defenses, and reached its initial objective. The Allies now controlled the plain south of the Sele River and the high ground an average of five miles from the beaches.[4]

The mountain village, Altavista, was taken in the original push from the beach. Germans troops quickly regrouped however, and punched their way back into town. The Division pulled back its defense along the rim of the landing area. Cecil would not have time to write for several days as every soldier who could be spared from field ranges, typewriters and trucks was on the line September 13. T-Patchers sealed off the Nazi's and drove off the lumbering Panzers. Covered by naval and land guns, the Texans rolled the enemy back into the hills. Altavista was retaken. Charles E. "Commando" Kelley was one of several who were awarded medals and citations at Salerno.

Cecil was with the Headquarters Artillery Battery when they came ashore to coordinate use of the big guns through radio communication with other units. The artillery's role was also noted in the official report on the success in the battle for Altavista:

> Late 17th of September the 36th Div Arty was supporting the 504th in Altavista by firing a concentration of 420 rounds every ten minutes and continued the harassment all night last night. Report from Col. Tucker, 504th Regt, was to effect that the arty fire was materially helping him hold out and was devastating to the Germans. A German officer captured . . . mentioned the (devastation) . . . wanted to know what kind we were firing. They still fear our artillery very much.[5]

Not many days after landing on Italian soil, the Texans managed to hold a church service not far from the front. It might seem incredible that the effort was made and time was found to gather the grateful survivors. Instead of fewer church services in the hectic war years that followed, the desperate situations called for a diligence on the part of the chaplains and the faithful few. Cecil noted the attendance of more than just the regulars that Sunday. These men had been through the toughest days of their lives so far and they knew many more months loomed ahead. The church service had a big impact on Cecil who wrote a description that would later be published in the *Baptist Standard*. "Deacon" Turner, with just a high school education, painted a vivid picture that would make his English teacher proud.

A Service at the Front
Corporal Cecil Turner, Headquarters, 36th Division

It was a beautiful Sabbath morning. The slight chill of the night was already gone, chased away by the slow rising September sun. The huge white oxen milled around nibbling on the straw in the spacious barnyard where our radio station was set up. Just outside was a huge oak tree that must have towered 90 feet into the sky. Its lower branches spread almost straight out, forming an umbrella of shade. Around the few houses nearby, the fast chatter of Italians could be heard, as they walked around aimlessly, still dazed by the battle that had been fought right there on their farms, in their vineyards, yards, and even in their homes. I remember one outer door that had been riddled by small arms fire. Some Nazi sniper had been silenced in that home.

That was the picture I remember mentally of the scene of the first church service after the 36th Division artillery landed in the invasion of Italy. That's what I remember seeing as I walked over to join the group already assembling under the giant oak. The sturdy oak reminded me of the unshaken faith of those men who had walked safely "through the valley of the shadow." Safely they had lived through what many had termed, "All hell broke loose."

The singing was good that morning and the selections could have been the same as some used in Texas Baptist churches that morning. The thanks the men had in the hearts could be read on their faces.

All were in a worshipful attitude. Some who weren't in the habit of attending church regularly were there. One fellow had volunteered to take my place at the radio so I could go to church.
The empty 155 millimeter shell crates made good benches, and their number was evidence of the long, fierce struggle just moved on.

Now and then a squadron of Spitfires or our P-51's roared over, stopping the sermon momentarily. Several times our gun batteries fired a volley, causing us to miss a few words of the chaplain's message. I felt a great responsibility when asked to word a prayer for that group of men. Who could know what was in their hearts? I remember asking the Lord to help us to continue successful if it were His will. I thought of the families of the fellows who wouldn't be going back with us. I hoped that someone would be able to help each relative with: "All things work together for good to them that love. . . ."

As we scattered, each man back to his post, there was one Scripture that came to me. It was in 1 Sam. 14:6, "And Jonathan said to the young man who bore his armor, 'Come, and let us go over unto the garrison of these uncircumcised: it may be that the Lord will work for us: for there is no restraint to the Lord to save by many or by few.'" The Lord had worked with us. Against tremendous odds we had invaded foreign soil, established a foothold, and advanced steadily. All who had attended that service must have realized there is One who is more powerful than tanks and guns.[6]

The command post was located at the base of Mt. Soprano. Headquarters, 36th Division Artillery set up their radio station nearby as well. The lines of support to the new front had been established and mail was now getting through. There had been no time for writing letters this past month, but Cecil could finally sit down a few minutes to let his family know he was safe. He could not tell them where he was nor did he want them yet to know all he had seen and lived through. He wrote mainly to reassure them of his condition. However, the therapeutic benefits of talking to his family through his pen always boosted his spirits. The reader can guess from the letters that his family thought it was time for Cecil to be coming home.

Cecil Turner operating radio at Headquarters, 36th Division Artillery.

Somewhere Outside the United States
September 28, 1943

My Dear Dad & Mom,

I received a letter yesterday from you written August the 29 and one from Veltie Sept. the first. I am doing all right and one of the things I dreaded most of all has been no worry at all. I have had plenty of food and water. Last nite for supper I'll bet I had just as good a meal as you did regardless of where you ate. We sure can appreciate the fighting Quartermaster Corps.

Well, we can dream I guess but maybe you had better not look for me back by the first of the year. That is crowding things a little maybe. I'm afraid I won't quite make it back for Christmas this year. Your letters are always an inspiration and I always look forward to your paragraph, Dad, at the last. Veltie is very good to write me. I must write him tomorrow. Always think of me when you pray and ask the Lord to lead us in every move we make. I hope and long for the day when we have triumphed over wrong and we can all be together again. Good luck to you and I'll tell you the rest after the war. Say hello to everybody for me and remember I am OK.

Love,
Cecil

Cecil snaps a shot of his buddies enjoying the K-rations at camp.

There was no doubt in his mind that this was a war against evil. However, Cecil knew that being in the right was not always synonymous with success. He knew they would need God's guidance in every move to win the battles ahead.

The 36th pulled back to establish defensive positions while other units seized Naples and drove the Germans several miles beyond. Casualties had been high for the Texas Division. The T-Patchers enjoyed a short rest as they waited for the reinforcements heading for Italy to boost their Division back to combat strength.

October 2, 1943

Dear Folks at home,

Having some pictures to send home and in order to have more space I am writing an air-mail letter. I am feeling good this afternoon. The afternoon has been mine to do anything I needed to do. A full night's sleep last nite is one of the reasons I feel so good.

There are a number of things I wish I could tell you and a lot of incidents I would like to describe but that must come after the war. We are getting a rest now and there's plenty of food. Let me tell you what dinner was like. A friend and I opened up two cans of meat & beans, put some green peppers that we got from some civilians and boiled some rice and put some sugar cubes in it. We have plenty of synthetic coffee so we made some in our canteen cups. We have a can that has little ration biscuits and three pieces of hard candy in each can. So you see we had a pretty good dinner.

I am so sorry to hear of Herman & Coney's home burning. I wonder how it started with such a headway. If they didn't even get out with their shoes it must have been far along when they awoke. Also, maybe that is something else we can thank the Lord for since they all got out safely. I will send them all the money I have now. I know the people will help them a lot but there are a lot of things that neighbors can't replace. Give them all of my love.

I had a nice letter from Irene and they are doing pretty good. She was so happy that Aubrey & Iona had accepted Christ and joined the church. Some of you must be guilty of not writing her, like I am–

(Three hours later) I have just received a letter from Mozelle, one from you, Mom, dated Aug. 14, and one from my dream girl in Merkel.

You might be able to read more in the newspaper and in magazines like Life, Time, Newsweek, and other news magazines than I can write in my letters. The Baptist Standard gets through pretty good. The Chaplain gets them often. The Roscoe Times hasn't arrived yet but it will. I'll enjoy it regardless of how old it is. (Goodnight see you in the morning)

Good morning. It's Sunday so I'll finish this letter then go to Church.

The soil is almost identical to the soil we have there at home. We are camped in a wheat field. I hooked to a plow the other day with a small caterpillar and plowed a little just for meanness.

I hear the Texas papers know where we are so watch for articles. I'll say this much. The 36ᵗʰ has kept up its great reputation and tradition.

Always pray for us—never forget. Pray that we may continue to succeed in a war against wrong—"I will fear no evil for Thou art with me."

Love,
Cecil

The loss of his sister's home would have seemed a great tragedy at any other time. Though Cecil had great sympathy for all they had lost, it must have paled in comparison to the life and death struggle that filled his days. He lived out the Scripture which urges us to "in everything give thanks" (1 Thessalonians. 5:18, KJV) and was very grateful his big sister's life had been spared. In quoting Psalms 23 the second time, Cecil may have revealed the chapter that became his heart's cry for the next two years as he walked "through the valley of the shadow of death" (KJV).

Telegrams were a quick method to keep his parents from worrying when duties kept him from finding time to write.

WESTERN UNION
N J Turner Box 236 Roscoe Texas.

Greetings from us all my thoughts are with you all my love
Cecil Turner
833am Oct 13 1943

"Deacon" Turner at the radio surrounded by exhausted troops.

October 17, 1943

Dear Dad,

Maybe it's about time I wrote you a letter—one just to you again. I know I haven't been writing very many letters home lately but enough to let you hear once and awhile and to know that I am OK. It has only been about two weeks since I heard from you and Mom. Had a letter yesterday from Coney but it was an old one—Aug 20.

Dad, you should see me under one of these apple trees over here. Big delicious apples and the trees have to be propped up they are so heavy. They are sure good, tree ripened. Can't eat over three at once!

The Sept. 27 Life magazine has some interesting pictures in it about the war. You can tell Veltie maybe he can find an old one.

Maybe I will send another box home soon if possible. We are still resting up. Keep writing and pray for us and say one especially for me. Hello Mom & all the rest.

Love,
Cecil

Six weeks after the invasion it was now safe to let his family know where he was. The propped up apple trees were in not-so-sunny Italy near Pazzuroli. Still no details of the battles could be given, but Cecil was very proud of the blows his Army and Division had dealt the enemy.

Many of Cecil's letters were written on Sunday when he might have had some time before or after church services. His buddies on the radio unit with him were good to let him trade off so he could have time to worship with other believers. Some Sundays he was Catholic and Protestant so he could take advantage of both services offered.

24 OCT 43
Somewhere in Italy

Dearest Mom & Dad,

This is Sunday afternoon and I'm feeling OK.—Went to both church services this morning.

I got a letter from Veltie with three pictures in it. They were sure interesting–some I sent from Africa to him.

I'm OK in every way. The rest I say after the war.

All my love,
Cecil

Deacon Turner had seen a lot of action but could not tell the extent of the danger to his worried parents. He was in the precarious position of wanting his family to know how desperately he needed prayer without worrying them. Years later in his fifties, Cecil would write in his journal:

> Prayer is the reach that man has been given that is limitless.
>
> Prayer worries the devil more than any human enterprise.
>
> Prayer is the opposite of worry.
>
> Prayer turns the battle over to God.
>
> You and I didn't think of prayer—God did.

"Call unto me, and I will answer thee, and show thee great and mighty things, which thou knowest not."

Jeremiah 33:3 (KJV)

Do you have a limitless reach in prayer?

Cecil hoped his family would be faithful to exercise their reach of prayer on his behalf.

4 Nov 43
Somewhere in Italy

Dearest Mom & Dad,

I received your letter of Oct. 20 and I was glad to hear that both of you are OK. Things are alright with me. Your letters may all be getting through. I don't know but I get one from you fairly often. If you care to start numbering them then you can find out how many I get. I would write you about the ones that were missing.

As you probably know we were the first American troops to hit European soil. "We let them have both barrels." I went to the front only once, the rest of the time I was back with our headquarters. I told Veltie about a couple of incidents that might be of interest to you. I have been in air raids that make any display of fireworks look small. A Nazi plane falling in flames at night makes quite a picture. The Germans are lousy shots and they are afraid of our crack shots.

That's all I think of today. I told Veltie I wanted a fur-lined fox hole for Xmas. Say hello to everybody–Bro. Elrod too.

Your roaming boy–
Love–Cecil

Once more, pride in the accomplishments of the 5th Army came through. The front was advancing as the 36th continued to rest and regroup. Cecil enjoyed the people and places of Italy but knew there were bitter days ahead fighting the cold and the Nazis.

13 Nov 43
Somewhere in Italy

Dearest Mom & Dad,

The nice Christmas package that you mailed in Sept. came today and I think it was real nice. The candy with nuts and candy syrup in it was real good. I really appreciate the camera film too. You can thank Wade for me. You remember there are some old ruins in Italy that would be good picture subjects. I have taken one roll already that I wouldn't take for. Let me say again that I really liked the box. Ava sent me a box of chocolates in a cellophane sealed tin box. Boy! Were they good. I am going to repay her and ask her to repeat the gift as often as possible.

There is nothing I can tell you interesting this time. I am doing OK. I got the Roscoe Times the other day so I guess I will be getting them regularly now. Thanks for the Times too. I can keep up with people that I know. I must send some of the nice little things of Italy when I get time. I must write Cassie and Irene. I got a letter from both of them. I'll eat a piece of candy and go to bed. Always anxious to see if you write a note on each letter, Dad.

All my love,
Cecil

Casualties and reinforcements had reduced the percentage of Texan T-Patchers to less than half of the Division makeup. However, the Division continued to fly the Lone Star flag over areas acquired and enjoyed the reputation of being the tough Texas bunch. On November 15, 1943, in the lower Liri Valley just north of Venafro, their rest ended. The 36th returned to the front lines and relieved the 3rd Infantry Division. The T-Patchers began "one of the most grueling and vicious campaigns in the history of modern warfare."[7]

At the end of the campaign, Major General Fred Walker, 36th Division Central Command, wrote:

> While subject to hardships that have never before been exceeded by any troops anywhere, you drove the enemy from well-organized and stoutly defended positions in the hill masses of Camino and Sammucro, Maggiore, Mount Rotundo, and San Pietro. You punished him severely.[9]

The frequent rain since their arrival on D-Day made the ground muddy and movement difficult. Sloping terrain made maneuvering even more challenging. However, the natural camouflage and protection from enemy artillery and aircraft made the area desirable. From November 15 to November 30, 1943, the 36th Division recorded the only 15 days of active duty in which they incurred no casualties.

21 Nov 43
Somewhere in Italy

My dear Dad,

It is time again for me to write again to just you and no

one else. Tell Veltie, Hubert, Auti and all I will write them as soon as I have time. By now you and Mom have gotten my last letter thanking you for the nice box.

Dad, I bet this is the first time you ever had a son to pause in time of war to write you a letter. I am on the radio tonite and there is not much traffic right now. You should have seen me the other nite bathing my poor thumb in wine which I heated with a candle. I couldn't get any water just then so wine had to do. Hot bathing does wonders for infection so my thumb is nearly well. You and Veltie would have gotten a laugh out of what I saw yesterday. An Italian showed me a secret room where he hid everything from the Germans. It was upstairs and he plastered over a door leading into a secret room. I sure laughed and he said in broken English, "Me Smart man."

I sincerely hope that you and mom are OK. It's nearly daybreak and I wish I could put my feet under your breakfast table but we will have to finish this job first.

Always remember me in your prayers.
Love,
Cecil

Raised in a Baptist home in a "dry" Texas county, Cecil was not a drinking man, nor would he become one. In war-torn Italy, however, wine served many purposes. Fresh, clean water was hard to find and to drink from the local sources could prove hazardous to one's health. Cecil was introduced to wine as a necessity and found other uses for it as well. He developed a taste for some of the better products of the vineyards in Italy and France. Later, Cecil was even bold enough to mention the possibility of bringing some home.

Word of the Italian invasion quickly spread back to the United States and slowly the details of the landing was making headlines. Someone received a copy of the following article and entered it into National Archives along with the Official After Action Reports from World War II.

November 24, 1943
Daily News–New York City
36th Division Joins U.S. Fighting Heroes

With the V Army in Italy, November 24 (AP) there is another star in the flag of Texas today. It was emblazoned there September 9, when the V Army landed on the shores of Italy. The first troops to hit the beach that thunderous morning wore T-Patches on their shoulders. The letter "T" stood for Texas and the patch for the 36th Division.

The Division was identified officially today. Now the story of the 36th can be told and nowhere in the military history of the United States is there a finer one.

It was an untried division in combat. Throughout the Army it was known as a "hot" outfit, however, and had distinguished itself time and time again in maneuvers. Originally it had been slated for a major role in the North African landing, but it was held back for something bigger.

The 36th came ashore in the Gulf of Salerno at dawn September 9. Days before, the 16th Panzer Division had moved into position. The Germans were ready and waiting. The 36th hit hard but it hit a strong wall. The first assault wave was pinned down with machine gun fire. The second and third waded ashore through a hail of bullets and shells. It looked for a time as though none of the three waves would be able to breach the German shore defense. Finally the Division broke through. For sheer courage in the face of withering fire, their attack at that moment rivals the greatest actions of American troops in any of our wars. Their first objective was a railroad line about 1000 yards from shore, and once off the beach they roared straight across fields through marshlands until they reached it.

German artillery in the hills a few miles back began shelling the beach. For perhaps a half an hour the battle hung in the balance.

At this moment, the commanding general and his staff waded through the surf, crossed the beach and made their way through the hottest part of the action to the railroad where the general took personal command of the action and the division held on.[10]

Everything surrounding Cecil had changed so drastically the past two years; it was somehow consoling that there was still normality at home. Getting the *Roscoe Times* gave him hope that his favorite part of the world was not yet torn up by this war, and his job was to see that it didn't spread that far.

Nov 30 - 43

Dearest Mom & Dad,

I got the papers mailed this morning to you Dad, and I hope it doesn't take as long for you to get them as it took them to get to me. I got a letter from Joyce written while she was there and all of you were OK then. A box arrived yesterday from Veltie, Hubert, & family. I guess everyone will be wanting to know whether their box arrived or not. Up to now there has been the one from you, mom, with the film in it from Wade. Two real nice ones from Ava, Some real nice candy and stuff from Auti & Agnes, the box from Hubert & Veltie, and so far I guess that's all. I wish I knew what to write that would interest you. It's always the same thing. I am OK, still a radio operator and I am even operating right now in the back of a truck tonite. I heard the news on a short wave set, from England tonite. I know that everything is OK at Roscoe now because I get the Roscoe Times—Thanks.

Goodnight, and always remember me when you pray. I'm always very glad to hear from home.

Love,
Cecil

Cecil's artillery unit was on the move much of the time, therefore, it was a vast improvement to operate the radio out of a two and one half ton truck. His responsibilities and work on the vehicle would escalate as the war waged on. He became such a fan of the army truck and Jeep, he later hinted at wanting one for the farm in Texas.

The Massachusetts communities had welcomed and claimed the 36th while they trained at Camp Edwards. Many in Cape Cod watched the war with special interest in where their Texans were and how they were faring in the war. The Camp Edwards experience had welded a link between these friendly Yankees and their Southern friends.

From a September 24, 1943 editorial in the *Falmouth Enterprise*, Falmouth, Mass by George A Hough, Jr.:

Our Texans at Salerno

A few months ago we were wondering when the 36th Division would go overseas, speculating why this long-trained outfit remained at Edwards while transports carried thousands of other men to the battlefronts. Our speculation was spurred by our experiences with the 36th.

We enjoyed many of the officers and their families who lived in the villages with us. We profited by the number of them who patronized our stores. And we observed that this outfit was lean and toughened and, by and large, ready for any kind of scrap. We had moments of feeling that much good scrapping spirit was being frittered away on Cape Cod.

Now Germany tells us the 36th landed at Salerno. American News dispatches tell us Texans have distinguished themselves in hard fighting at the beachheads. We can say, "I told you so." Falmouth never doubted that the 36th would hold its own in any kind of rough house.

We said goodbye to the 36th with mingled emotions of relief and regret. We knew then we would never entertain another such bunch. And chances are we never will.

... Many outfits have moved in and out of Camp Edwards since. None has caused the commotion, made the impression which the 36th brought. Of course we are interested in news of the 36th from Italy. Of course we'll watch its fighting prowess. Our Texas visitors were as much Texans when they left as when they came. We may be pardoned for observing that we remained Cape Codders. Still, a link was forged, perhaps a stronger link because of the differences it encompassed. Many of our Texans said they'd come back to see us after the war. We want to see them back.[11]

Newt was gradually phasing out of farming himself and wanted to be sure that his land would pass to the next Turner generation. Deeding his son some land was probably an act of faith and encouragement to Cecil. In essence, his father was saying, "You have some land waiting for you *when* you come home."

Nov. 30, 1943
Somewhere in Italy

Dearest Dad,

I received the papers about a week ago but am just now getting the time to get them signed and sent back. Let me know if you deed anything to me and I will make a will of some kind in case I get snake bitten over here.

I had better go eat breakfast so be good and let me hear from you often. I am OK. Will write tomorrow.

All my love,
Cecil

Cecil did not mind using the word "death" when he talked to his brother about needing a will, but once again, he would not alarm his father with the grim possibility. It was easier to joke about getting "snake bit."

As the war continued to heat up, the temperature

continued to drop. Few exact temperatures are in the official record, but it does mention the need for more wool socks and requested 6,000 be sent—- priority status. The enemy would have to be pushed out field by field and hill by hill. The Germans with their advantageous hilltop positions had full observation of the advancing Allies in the valleys below. The early adrenalin rush with the victorious landing was wearing off. The reality of the months and years required to finish the job was sinking in.

30 Nov 43

Dear Veltie & family,

So Ronny is talking right along now, huh? Wish I could see the little fellow! The box you and Hubert sent was good, peanut candy, etc. Where did you get it? I have about 10–11 rolls of film taken now and waterproofed.

I sent the power of attorney paper back this morning. If Dad deeds anything to me let me know. Let me know how it reverts back in case of my death. I want to make a will if it's a normal deed.

I'm feeling a little down hearted tonite so my letter won't be much. I am always OK I guess I am getting a little weary of the war. If you ever see any wool sox about an inch thick and a pair of lined long calf gloves you can buy me some and also a bottle of Murine, Vitalis, chocolate covered peanuts, hard chocolates at Woolworth's, etc. "Don't want much do I?" I'll be sending more stuff home when I get time off. Wish I could send a bottle of this Italian wine. Hello Doris!

Love,
Cecil

Finding time and light before bedtime to write to those at home. (Cecil at left)

Among Cecil's letters and pictures were some long sheets containing a short personal log. Included were some dates, a short entry of locations and sometimes a quick word or two to jog his memory of what happened there. For November 11, 1943 he wrote, "Piccili, long stay, million dollar hill." The artillery expenditure earned the target its popular name. Six hundred Allied guns attacked the hill above Camino-Maggiore which guarded the Mignano Gap. Continual rains turned the mountainside into a slippery, treacherous obstacle. On Thanksgiving Day, the men came down briefly from the rocky ledges to enjoy a hot turkey meal.

5 Dec '43
Somewhere in Italy

My dear Dad & Mom,

I received your letter of Nov. 18 today. I am answering because both of you make me feel that you do want to hear from me often. I thought maybe an occasional note now and then would be all you would care for or expect. Maybe you would like to hear as often as I like to hear from home. Anyway, I will try to write almost every day if I can regardless of where I am. I received a letter today from Coney and a copy of the Roscoe Times. I had to laugh out when I read where Jameson shot himself accidentally. He should just carry a club or cap pistol. I am doing OK tonite and getting plenty to eat. We had fried chicken for supper tonite and, boy was it good! When you hear that I am coming home, get a frying size chicken just for me.

That's all for tonite. I'll go to bed.

Think of me and pray we may still be successful.
Love,
Cecil

He sounded like a typical twenty-five year old that would laugh out loud at an accidental shooting and kid about limiting the boy to carrying a club. His love of fried chicken was also typical of Texas farm boys.

In all the requests for prayer, Cecil never mentions how fervently his own prayers pleaded for victory and personal safety. It seems unlikely, however, that he could be such a believer in prayer and not spend time himself communicating with God. He also knew the Bible proclaimed the prerequisite for having effective prayers was a righteous life. He would need a pure life to stand before God and ask for success over their enemy. Forty years later he would write, "Our spiritual level never rises above our praying. Our praying never rises above our spiritual level."

Mt. Maggiore had been taken, but the enormous problem of maintaining the position over the extended single line of supplies had begun. Heavy German artillery pounded the newly won positions of the supply line. For another week, the men endured more rain and enemy shells until relief could be sent. This came in the novel attempt of dropping supplies by a fighter plane to the hungry Texans on the mountain. These good intentions fell short and the Germans enjoyed the K-rations.

7 Dec 43

Dearest Mom & Dad,

It's nite again and I have time to write you again.

Two years ago I was home for the weekend from Camp Bowie. Dec. 7 a date that will make Japan unpopular for a long time. Sometimes the time seems short that I have spent in the Army and sometimes it seems ages. Almost three years I have spent of the best part of my life. I only hope we accomplish more by winning this war than we did in the last. I hope that my son, if any, will not have to go through all of this like I have. More than ever I realize that we have more than anyone to fight for. Outside of the Americas and the British Empire there is no civilization.

I wonder what you two would be doing if it were the same time there as it is here. Maybe you would be in a domino game and I could sneak in and raid the refrigerator for a glass of milk and a piece of cold baked pork loin. It's time for me to wake up the next shift so, goodnight and good luck.

Lovingly,
Cecil

As Cecil heard of friends getting married and new babies being born into the family, it made him wonder where he would be right now if the war had not called him. This was the best part of his life—when decisions to marry, have kids, and buy a home come tumbling at a young man. Life seemed to be passing him by. Cecil was still a boy in many ways when he left for boot camp. After the grueling experiences he had already endured, he was gaining the strong opinions of a man. His experience in North Africa and in Italy so far had made even country living in Roscoe, Texas, look like the center of human civilization. He had a new, deeper appreciation for the prosperity and freedoms he had taken for granted. However, just the thought of a cold glass of milk and Cecil was back to the big kid who would sneak into the kitchen to raid the refrigerator.

9 Dec 43

Dearest Dad & Mom,

I am doing fine on this pretty moonlight nite. It's about two o'clock in the morning. I'll bet it's cold in Texas tonite but it's only a little cool here sometimes. It will soon be Christmas. I wish I could send a lot of the walnuts that are so plentiful in Italy especially back at the apple orchard that I mentioned once before. The Italians would come by selling them. Everyone had walnuts. A steel helmet full for about 25 cents usually.

I got a nice letter from Ava & Coney today. It sounds as though Howard will go overseas again. I wonder if he will go back into the Pacific theatre or some other war zone. Ava sent me the cutest picture of Clay Jr.! Coney seems to like her new home pretty well. She got the money I sent her. When you write her always tell her how much I love her and how much I am concerned about their making good in their new location. I do hope they can start saving for their future security. Goodnight,

Love,
Cecil

9 Dec '43

Dearest Mom & Dad,

The little fruit cake got here today. It was in good shape as most all of the Xmas packages have been. Boy! Was it good. I hardly see how so much goodness could have been packed in one cake. I appreciate it very much. I am going to even put the metal box into use. I'll fill it with little things of mine and put it under the seat of my truck. I probably didn't tell you I drive our radio truck now. That's one of my additional duties. There are ten of us in the radio section and we have a 2 ½ ton truck. You have seen a lot of them. They have eight wheels behind and front wheel drive for the two in front to be used in mud. It has five more speeds forward. I pull a trailer too with about 2 thousand pounds on it. That's all I know tonite so I'll go to bed. Looks like I'll get more sleep tonite than usual. Tell everyone hello for me.

Love,
Cecil

For the rest of his life, Cecil adored fruitcake. The memory of the wonderful dessert his family sent may have been exaggerated over the years, as he remembered how fantastic the special treat tasted that cold Italian Christmas. The colorful tin was put to use and was a reminder of home every time he reached under the truck seat.

The truck Cecil and the radio crew manned raised them a step up from the life the foot soldier endured. He probably volunteered to drive in order to escape the bumpy benches back in the bed of the vehicle. Driving the truck in the Liri Valley was no picnic, however, with the lack of roads, mud up to the axle, and enemy fire from surrounding rocky hillsides. At least the driver was afforded the luxury of enduring the bumpy hours on a padded seat. Some health problems later in life could be traced to the hours and days spent jostling around in that truck.

12 Dec '43

Dearest Mom & Dad,

This is Sunday noon so I will write before I go to eat. We had Church this morning in a cave dug into solid rock. You should see the testament Mae Wheeler sent me. It is pocket size and has a metal armor plate on one side that is gold colored.

I am on duty at our radio station and telegraph sets today as usual.

So Joyce Elrod got married. I'll have to take her name off my list. Ha! Joyce was always a very good friend of mine. I may try to buy her something nice here in Italy and send it to her if I find out where she is living.

I'll bet you two will be busy in the yard now that you have a new home. I wish I could have seen the old place last Spring & Summer. It must have been pretty. Always anxious to hear from you.

Your far away -
Cecil

Deacon Turner continued attending church whenever possible—even in a cave! The days ahead would cause him to call on his faith to deal with all he would see and endure. The Division spread their attack over Mt. Defensa and Mt. Lungo in the first week of December. Before Christmas, the 36th fought over more mountains and the valley villages below. Mt. Sammucro, which towered 4,000 feet above San Pietro in the valley below, had rocky slopes so steep the Texans had to use their ropes as lassos to pull themselves over the otherwise impossible cliffs. Supplies had to be carried up by pack horses, mules and humans, then casualties were borne back down the same way. The freezing temperatures and short supplies of coats and blankets resulted in the comparison of this period to the physical discomforts of Washington's army at Valley Forge.

Battalions of the 36th moved through the valley attacking the German-held town of San Pietro on December 15, 1943. The enemy had dug in with well-armed pill boxes and barbed wire. All 5th Army artillery within range was directed against San Pietro and the surrounding area. The 1,400 villagers had been liberated, but at a cost of 1,400 casualties from the Texans. The battle was immortalized in the film, *San Pietro*, by director (Major) John Huston. Cecil only hints at the action he had seen.

15 Dec '43
ITALY

Dearest Mom & Dad,

My thoughts go back to you tonite there at home. How are you, tonite?

I received a letter from Coney and one from Cassie yesterday. Things are the same with me. I hear the news pretty regular now. I read where the bill for servicemen mustering out pay was being considered again. They were considering 200 to 500 dollars.

I saw a real XXXXX Nazi plane being hit and it fell straight down and went up in flames.

Are you keeping a cow now, Dad, and how about chickens? I won't know what to do every morning if there's no cow to milk.

I'm getting a treat now and then when one of the fellows gets a box from home. We divide up and that way we get something good often. Yesterday I got a chocolate bar. I am doing fine and am comparatively safe all the time. Say hello to the people we know. Write to your Italian son–

Love,
Cecil

To avoid writing an absolute lie to his father, Cecil used the word "comparatively" in assuring his safety at this point. The central command had positioned itself further up the valley at Venafro.

19 Dec 43

Dearest Mom & Dad,

This is Sunday afternoon and it's a pretty day. I'm writing while I operate a radio. We had Church again this morning and sang a few Christmas songs. I am sure missing the type of Church service that we have in Texas.

The box of chocolate fudge came yesterday and it was in good shape. It apparently has lost none of its goodness and flavor. It was very nice–Thank you!

The wheat must be pretty by now. Veltie told me he had 140 acres of wheat up.

My last letter from Joyce was written Nov. 5. She wanted me to write more often. You write and say hello for me. I won't be able to write real often. Maybe Ava is back now.

I'm OK and I hope everything is alright with you. Don't work too hard!

Love,
Cecil

Christmas overseas was the toughest time to be so far from Cecil's loved ones and the tree they would gather around. With packages of homemade Texas fudge and fruitcake, his family helped him through this first holiday season on foreign soil. Singing some Christmas carols helped, but how he missed being in his home church in Roscoe.

23 Dec 43

Dearest Mom & Dad,

I got your last letter yesterday dated Nov. 2 but I know you meant Dec. 2 because of other dates you mentioned. Was it the elderly Mr. Gracy who was buried? I got a letter yesterday from you, Bobbie Wash, Joy Boles, Roberta & Pat, Veltie, and a real nice box of chocolates from Ava. She is the sweetest one.

Things aren't so bad with me. I won't have such a tough Christmas. Like Roberta said, we get busy doing things and forget to dislike it. One can get used to a lot.

You mentioned my sending my film home and you could maybe send me some more. Right now regulations prevent my sending them home. I have a total of 13 rolls of exposed film. Maybe soon I can send them home. I have four rolls to take yet. Ten rolls of mine were given to me and I don't know what all he took with them.

Happy holidays and always be cheerful.
Your son,
Cecil

In Cecil's journal he makes the note that he didn't have to dream of a white Christmas in 1943. He was near the village of Venafro on December 25th and woke up to a blanket of snow. That would be a treat in a warm house in Roscoe, Texas. With few coats and blankets, the snow was not a welcome sight to most of the cold-weary Texans.

Four months prior, Cecil had probably never seen a dead man. Casualties had been high in the December struggle. One regiment alone required 1100 replacements in order to build back up to the 2500 men it needed. It must have seemed at times, as the bodies kept coming into the headquarters, that the dead might outnumber the survivors. Cecil could not endure so much death around him without intensifying his feelings toward the Germans. His new attitude toward his fellow man must have been hard to justify next to the loving standards with which he had been raised. For the remainder of the war, he wrestled with the evil the Germans had inflicted and the German people themselves.

Famous war correspondent, Ernie Pyle, endured the winter battles with the 36th Division. The G.I.'s loved him because he gave the folks back home a vivid picture of the "doughboy's" war in Italy. Cecil was at Venafro, at the base of Mt. Sammucro, the same time Pyle saw the mule trains carry casualties down the mountain. Of all the dispatches the correspondent filed over the years, the touching story of Captain Waskow from Belton, Texas, is perhaps the best known:

> I was at the foot of the mule train the night they brought Capt. Waskow's body down the mountain . . . Dead men had been coming down the mountain all evening, lashed onto the backs of mules . . . The Italian mule-skinners were afraid to walk beside dead men so Americans had to lead the mules down that night . . . You feel small in the presence of dead men, and ashamed of being alive . . . Four mules stood there, in the moonlight, in the road where the trail comes off the mountain. The soldiers who led them stood there waiting. "This one is Capt. Waskow," one of them said quietly. Two men unlashed his body from the mule and lifted it off and lay it in the shadow beside the low stone wall.

. . . a soldier came and stood beside the officer, and bent over, and he spoke to his dead captain, not in a whisper but awfully tenderly, and he said: "I sure am sorry, sir."

Then the first man squatted down and he reached down and took the dead hand, and he sat there for a full five minutes, holding the dead hand in his own and looking intently into the dead face, and never uttered a sound all the time he sat there.

And then finally, he put the hand down, and then reached up and gently straightened the points of the captain's shirt collar, and then he sort of rearranged the tattered edges of his uniform around the wound. And then he got up and walked away down the road in the moonlight, all alone.[12]

It was a sad time for all GI's when Ernie Pyle was killed later in the Pacific. Many who never met him felt they had lost a close friend.

Cecil rarely discussed those that died on the battlefield. He noted several in his worn journal. Forty years later, in a message to some prison inmates, Cecil was explaining how Christ gave His life so that we might be saved. He recounted the story of a soldier named Willie Lott who gave his life to save others. This sacrificial conduct warranted enduring tribute by Cecil and no doubt others who witnessed such unselfishness.

28 Dec 43
In Sloppy Italy

Dearest Mom & Dad,

Here's a few lines before I go to bed. I have been doing swell lately. I have been near a fellow from Merkel for the past few days. He knows all the people that I know there–even my girl, Louise.

I saw several good Germans today the only good ones I have ever seen (dead ones).
If you ever see anything in the papers about us that you don't like just take for granted that it isn't true.

Hey! Dad, where do you hunt jackrabbits now? Don't let the old shotgun rust.

If all of the bonuses pass the House and Senate maybe I will loan you some money when I get home.

The only thing you have to worry about is whether I get lots of letters or not. That's all for now.

Love,
Cecil

Turner was expert at completely escaping the war in his letters. Once his pen was in hand, he could talk about Merkel and jackrabbits and be far away from the dead, the noise and the cold in war-torn Italy.

3 Jan 44

Dearest Mom & Dad,

I am on the telegraph tonite so I will write you even though it is in the dead of nite. I had a swell dinner yesterday, turkey with all the trimmings.

I would be plenty sore if I thought any of you ever worried about me. I am doing OK.

I am about ready for a nice long letter from somebody giving me the details of everything that is going on at home. The Roscoe Times has been coming pretty good.

How are things selling now in Texas? What did you pay for the Prasser home? What can you get for your tractor?

Let me know when the war will be over and I can come home from it all.

I love you,
Cecil

In several letters, Cecil referred to the sloppy conditions in Italy. It rained daily for seventeen days when they re-entered the line in the Mignano-San Pietro sector. His radio truck wallowed and stalled in axle-deep mud. Of this time period and the battles and winter months that lay ahead, General Walker at their conclusion would justifiably state:

> I do not recall any campaign in the whole history of the United States Army in which soldiers have had to endure greater hardships or have per-

formed greater deeds of heroism than this campaign in Italy.[13]

By the end of December, the valley up to Venafro was secure and the Texans could enjoy their second turkey meal in Italy. The Division once again shifted briefly into reserve status. The weariness in Cecil's letters confirms several accounts concerning the T-Patch troops. Many historians have concluded that the 36th was "close to exhaustion" by the end of 1943.

7 JAN 44
In Sloppy Italy

Dear Mom & Dad,

Here's to let you know I am OK and feeling fine. By the way, I had a hot shower the other day. Was that a treat! I will get a number of your letters soon I guess. They haven't been coming so regular. Maybe they will all come in at once soon.

Every time I write a letter I wish I could tell you a few things interesting but there just isn't anything I can write. We are fighting the Germans in Italy as you read in the paper and that's all there is to it–we are winning!!!

Let me know if anything happens there and I will write everything I can from here.

Always glad to hear from home–
How is the wheat Dad?

Love,
Cecil

12 JAN 44
Sloppy Italy

Dear Mom & Dad,

I got a copy of the Roscoe Times, two letters from you, written Dec. 18 and 22, two letters from Joyce, one from Veltie, and one from Doris Lynn. HOW IS AVA?

You have gotten my other letters by now stating that I enjoyed the cake and the cigar box full of good home-made fudge. They both arrived about Xmas time. Thank you so much!

Do you live next door to the Haney's now in the little home B.B. Hamilton once lived in? If that is it I remember it as a cute little home. If you move anymore you had better put a name plate on the door so I can find it when I get back. (joke) Hey! Dad, what's this you said about worrying about me? I oughta' get a furlough and come home just to scold you for that. I am just as OK as can be. The Jerries [Germans] will have to do a lot better if they ever get me. The only thing I wonder about is what will become of me when the war is over–no shoes, no hat, no car, no suit, nothing but army shirts, no wheat, no cotton seed. (joke) I hope you enjoy this stuff I write. My spirits are always high.

I love you,
Cecil

Newt and Martha Turner with grandson, H. C. Boston, Jr.,
in front of their new house in town.

15 JAN "44
Italy

Dearest Dad & Mom,

*It's Saturday nite and I'll write a work before I go to bed.
I got two letters from you 25 and 26ᵗʰ of Dec. Ava was at
home and wrote a note.*

*Didn't Ava have a car? Does she still have it? Since there
is nothing else to write about I'll mention that I am now
an oatmeal eater. Tell Ava that she will have to wash the
sticky oatmeal out of the little stewer after breakfast, 'cause
if I have breakfast with her I must have my oatmeal.*

I guess little Howard Clay will have some neighbor kids to play with. Let me know when you hear from Howard. The war in the Pacific is looking better every day. Send me his address.

That's all tonite.

Love,
Cecil

After a short respite from action, units of the Texas Division obeyed their orders to undertake one of the most difficult and controversial of all military operations. In a questionable move that is still debated today, General Clark selected the 36th Division to undertake one of the most prohibitive of all military operations—crossing a strongly defended river at night. With little time to recover from their previous ordeal, the Lone Star Division was back in combat on January 20, 1943, with an assault on the Rapido River in the Cassino area. Within those first two days of attack, the Texans suffered 3,000 casualties. Weary, exhausted, with ammunition gone, men fought bravely until the weight of the German counterattacks forced a decision. The Rapido assault was a failure.

New York Times correspondent C. L. Sulzberg cabled this report:

When the 36th Division sought valiantly and vainly to establish itself across the icy Rapido River, it suffered losses that look heavy to American military history. It was the boys of the 36th who stumbled through night-screened minefields with assault boats on their shoulders and down to the Rapido—suffering immensely en route. It was the boys of the 36th who crawled across a thickly-iced rail-less bridge over a bloody little stream and fell under a hail of gun, mortar, and automatic fire in the gallant but vain attempt to establish a bridgehead.

They call the 36th the "hard luck" division because it has never had an easy assignment. This writer saw one of its battalions when what was left of it clamored back across the Rapido. They were tired but they remained, in essence, fresh-faced boys from Texas.[14]

Feelings ran high before and after the defeat concerning the wisdom of the order to cross the treacherous river. Mounting dissention led to an official Army investigation after the war. One last commentary on the Rapido tragedy is contained at the end of the official record filed by the officers:

In conclusion, I desire to invite attention to the fact that the Rapido River was strongly defended by a force equal in number, or superior to the attacking force. The first attack was made, under cover of darkness, but was unsuccessful. The British attack on the South, the previous night, had likewise been unsuccessful. An attack by the 34th Division to the North, on a subsequent night, was likewise unsuccessful. The last attack by this regiment was made in the daylight, which was furthermore, and more decisively unsuccessful. Losses from attacks of this kind are tremendous in manpower and material, and in addition have a devastating demoralizing effect upon those few troops who survive them. Officers and men lost in the Rapido River crossing cannot be replaced, and the combat efficiency of a regiment is destroyed. If we continue to gamble against odds with the German Army, it is my opinion we will greatly assist him in his efforts to defeat us. It has been said that success in battle depends upon the leadership of commanders. It can be truthfully said that as long as leaders who have the guts to plunge into hopeless odds such as this operation and are sacrificed like cannon fodder, our success in battle will suffer in proportion and disaster will eventually come.

William H. Martin
Colonel, 143rd Infantry,
Commanding.[15]

Cecil wrote home the day after the initial defeat at Rapido. He continued to reassure his family of his safety and only described one close encounter because he could joke about it lightheartedly. Perhaps his father began to assume (like the reader), that the more Cecil insisted that he was not in danger, the worse the situation must have been.

22 JAN '44

Dearest Mom and Dad,

Your letter of December 27 sent airmail arrived almost as soon as the V-Mail written Jan. 1st so when you want to write a long letter remember that it won't be but a few days longer getting here. I like V-Mail written often but an airmail to give the details of what is going on about every two weeks. Dad could write a whole page that way. Ha!

I am doing fine and dandy. The only time I have been sick was from breathing the fumes from a charcoal fire and that was about two months ago. I vomited until my tonsils almost came out. An interesting thing happened sometime ago. Ole Jerry was hurling little artillery at us. Three of us were under cover waiting for the firing to cease. Then came five shells whistling over, one right after the other. Four of them were "duds." They just rattled into the mud and were just like so many rocks thrown at us. That tickled the heck out of me and I laugh every time I think of it.

The box you are sending must be real nice. You included nearly everything I need. It should be here soon.–

Hello Ava & H.C. Jr. Everybody be good and think of me when you pray.

Your Italian son,
Cecil

The "duds" that came whistling over head could have been a life-threatening situation. Instead, Cecil saw the absurdity of shooting those shell "rocks" at them. Perhaps his humor was one way he was able to deal with the daily stress and danger.

22 JAN 44

Dearest Mom & Dad,

I thought you might want an answer to your letter of Dec. 27 which was almost all business. I wrote another letter this morning so I should have plenty of space in this one. As there was no questions in the letter to answer I will just say that anything you want to do will be all right with me. Dad, I know that you never did anything that I didn't think was alright unless there was a licking with a peach tree limb when I was a kid–Ha! If you want to give me something on the Veltie Place that is certainly alright with me. Anything you give me is probably more than I deserve. If and when I get back to the good ole USA, I will be so glad and thankful I will be satisfied with anything. To be back alive and well will be enough for me. I'll probably kiss the ground when I go ashore. I am sure that I will be anxious to get established financially before too long as that is important in anyone's life. Some people forget their future security which is tragic sometimes.

I'll write again soon.

Lovingly,
Cecil

23 JAN '44

Dearest Mom & Dad,

I am catching up on my letters to you so you will have to hurry to catch up.

I am sitting up tonight on the radio and feeling fine.

How is Ava and H.C.? I may have to run over and help Howard finish up when we get through over here. Tell Ava I am thanking her again for sending me the book "Silent Trumpet." It is one way of getting some of the fellows to read a little. It's a modern story of how a man of the world came to know Christ while he was in college.

That Ava is a sweet gal!

Say, in your last letter you said I had sent home $600. Has that much come in by check and money order? When the Jan. check from Washington ($40) arrived that should have been $510 total that I have sent home since I left. Maybe you were right. Maybe I have sent more than I remember. Are the $40 checks all coming in? Including Jan. there should be nine. Payday I'll send $100 more from here.

All of you must enjoy hearing the good news every nite from all fronts.

Love,
Cecil

Cecil was not the only active Christian reared in the Newt Turner home. Ava often played the piano at church and faithfully encouraged her little brother. Her husband, Howard, was fighting in the Pacific. She sent several boxes of goodies to the fronts in the East and West. Besides all the homemade treats and chocolates she shipped to Cecil, she helped him find a useful book to open the lines of communication with his foxhole friends about this God to whom he prayed.

Even though his unit had suffered a brutal defeat, Cecil managed to stay upbeat and optimistic about the war. He operated the telegraph as well as the radio and wrote the following message in telegraph style. It is amusing to note the censors removed the word "Rome" in the letter but left the segment identifying it as the city where Paul was imprisoned. Even readers with limited familiarity with the scriptures would know Paul's confinement was in Rome. However, we can generously assume the censors were Biblically literate; they were simply confident German intelligence would not catch the reference.

January 31, 1944
Italy

My dear Dad,

It is time once again for another one of those letters just for you alone. Every so often you remember I like to write a letter just to you. (STOP) Things are going alright with me, Dad, I am feeling fine these days and have no complaints. Don't ever get a chance to weigh but I think I'm as heavy as I ever get. (STOP) I am still operating radio and little telegraph now and then. I am on the radio tonite and can write you as there isn't much traffic. (STOP) Some day when we get into XXXX I will see if they have any records of where Paul was imprisoned until he died. There might be an accurate record of those things. (STOP) How is the wheat looking? How much did you plant this year? Did they allow you to plant all you cared to? (STOP) The Roscoe Times came the other day and I read about the meeting coming up. Was it a success? You may have to teach me a few manners when I get back, especially table manners. I have nothing but a spoon left. I get my ear wet even.
Dad, always pray for me when you talk to the Good Lord

Love,
Cecil

He would have heard the scolding all the way to Italy if they could have seen his newly acquired table manners in which even his ears got wet. It is surprising that the hint of lacking utensils did not trigger a package equipped with knife and fork. It did, however, trigger a smile on the faces of loved ones as must have been the intent.

February 1, 1944
Somewhere in Italy

Dearest Mom & Dad,

I got a letter from Ava today and one from Irene. Just in case Ava didn't get my last letter will you thank her for me. I got the 2 ½ lb. box of candy. Gee! It was sure nice! Tell her it was the one she sent Nov. 11, - the one that had 2 giant chocolate bars in it too. The one that all of you sent me will probably be here soon.

Things are alright with me as usual. Do any of the kids read any articles from Ernie Pyle. He is a war correspondent who is probably sending back plenty about the 36th.

We got paid today and I am sending this $100 money order you can deposit for me when you have time. A minute ago I figured up to see how much money I might have saved. If everything was there (all checks) on Feb. 10 I would have sent $610 total. I had $300 when I left–Veltie is using part of that which is alright. That totals $910.–not bad. I got the world news tonite short-wave from London.

I imagined that I could see you two getting the news over the big radio there at home. The news was good tonite from all fronts.

I have decided that after all of this I would like to lead a nice quiet life when I get home. I was having a talk with a friend of mine and he laughingly said he had been doing dangerous jobs all his life and when he went home he thought he would have him a florist shop when the war is over.

Say, Mom, would you do something for me? Some time when you are in Sweetwater will you get Ava something nice? She has been so nice to send me the candy which is so tasty when you have been eating stew and other greasy food. Dad can get the money at the bank out of my account and sometime when you are in Sweetwater you could get it. When I get a chance I am going to send some more little things from Italy. Wish I could send some of the souvenirs that the Germans leave around when they get off in a hurry.

Say hello to everyone for me and don't forget me when you pray.

Love,
Cecil

Perhaps because of the French that Cecil acquired while in North Africa, he was selected in early February to work as a liaison to the French Artillery in Italy. He stayed with them for most of the month while his Division kept trying to find a way through the Liri Valley, the door to Rome. Cecil was on the opposite hills where he had a bird's-eye view of the struggle below.

14 Feb '44

Dearest Mom & Dad,

It's been several days since I have had time to write but I am still OK. I am with a party of three and we are with the French. You no doubt have read of how the Americans, British, and French are cooperating to win the war. We represent the 36ᵗʰ Artillery at the French Artillery. The French are good soldiers.

I sincerely hope all of you are well and don't have the flu any more.

Keep writing to me—

Love,
Cecil

The other two from the 36th that worked with the French during February, 1944. (the one on the radio was Todd Mayne Jr.)

"Checking radio set and calling planes overhead.
Set I used while with the French."

19 Feb 44

Dearest Mom & Dad,

Once again I am in a hurry but can drop you a line. I am doing fine and still with the French.

The box with the gloves, sox, & candy arrived and there was a little snow on the ground when they got here. They are very nice and handy. The candy was very nice and delicious. Thanks! Will write again soon.

Love,
Cecil

22 Feb 44

Dearest Mom & Dad,

I received two letters yesterday–Jan. 31 and Feb. 8. I am still with the French. As I said before there are three of us who represent the 36th with a French division.

The information about my little bank account was what I wanted and was sufficient. You said $634 plus the two hundred Veltie is using is $834 plus the $100 I mailed the other day is $934. Anyway, I figure that is about right. I don't imagine anyone has checked on me except Veltie and that was OK. If it would help you to keep up with it you could have him always tell you when he writes a check. Where did the $37.93 come from? Don't know who would be sending an odd amount to my account. I will write more later about the nice box you sent. If that box could talk it could tell you some pretty good stories about the spot it was in. I am sure glad to hear that Hubert is better. I must go now.

Love,
Cecil

It is interesting that in the three previous letters the censor did not delete the referral to the liaison work with the French and yet in the fourth letter they did. The degree of censorship must have varied as greatly as the censors themselves.

Cecil's time with the French must have been intense, indicated by the infrequent letters and remark about "the spot" his box was in. He certainly would have many stories to tell about working with the French up in those hills. Cecil admired their ability but was counting the days until he could return to his old Battery.

25 Feb 44

Dearest mom & Dad & Ava,

I have no idea what day of the week this is but I know the date from my radio information. I am still with the XXXX and expect to go back to the 36th soon. I got the Roscoe Times again the other day and even though it was old it was interesting.

I have not received as many letters from Veltie as I usually do. Maybe because I have been too busy to write him often.

There isn't much to write but I wanted to let you hear from me while I had a little time to write. I sent two telegrams not long ago while I was busy and couldn't write. I have a number of experiences. I would relate if I were home.

I'm always anxious to hear from home. Did I see in the Baptist Standard where P.D. O'Brien was in Colorado now?

Love,
Cecil

Three days after writing this letter, Cecil made a choice that earned him a commendation. It was such a dangerous situation that he received a citation for meritorious conduct and he sent this telegram to let his unsuspecting family know he had survived. Although he did not hint at the peril earlier that day, his heartbeat was probably still racing while penning the words.

WESTERN UNION
N J Turner
Box 263 Roscoe Texas

Greetings all well and safe best wishes & good health
Cecil Turner
825am Feb. 28 1944

Although Cecil did not officially receive his commendation until five months later, the citation was awarded for his radio work and narrow escape with the French that day.

Commendation for Exceptionally
Meritorious Conduct

CECIL E. TURNER, Technician Fifth Grade, Headquarters Battery, 36th Division Artillery, for exceptionally meritorious conduct on 28 February 1944 in Italy. Tec 5 Turner was assigned as a radio operator on liaison duty, maintaining radio communication between Headquarters 36th Division Artillery and a French Corps Headquarters. When communication ceased to be available, Tec 5 Turner, against the advice of an officer, voluntarily maintained and repaired the wire communication between the two Headquarters, despite intense shelling and adverse weather. He made possible, through his courageous action and determination, the only communication by which the French Corps Headquarters could request artillery support from the 36th Division Artillery. Entered the Service from Abilene, Texas.

Deacon Turner at the radio

In many ways, letters and boxes from home formed a lifeline for the soldier. The package from home last month provided invaluable gloves to help Cecil string the communication wire that saved French lives. In early March, Turner headed back to his Headquarters Artillery Battery and to his waiting mail.

March 3, 1944

Dearest Mom & Dad, (and Ava) Somewhere in Italy

How are you? I'm OK.

I'll get my mail tomorrow so maybe I'll have a letter from you.

Let me tell you again how nice the box of candy, the gloves, and other things were. The gloves were just in time for a cool spell of weather. I have sure used them a lot since they got here, running telephone lines and such work as that. The Sox are very warm and also came in handy. Tell Veltie the Murine hit the spot and I will really make use of the Vitalis as soon as I can shampoo my hair. Maybe I mentioned that the box could tell quite a story if it could speak.

I get the Roscoe Times pretty often now. One got lost and came in late. It was a Dec. 3 issue coming in March. Ha! I see where the Locker plant must be well under construction now. We will kill a beef and freeze it. Remember I am a good butcher.

Love,
Cecil

One by one, depleted units of the 36th trickled off the line for a much-needed rest after the Cassino fiasco along the Rapido River. Arrival of replacements and retraining kept the entire Division out of combat through April. While commanders outlined impending strategies, GI's rested in the Maddaloni area and had front row seats to a spectacle most Texans will never see. GI's stood in awe as Mt. Vesuvius spurted forth its most violent eruption in 72 years. During windy March evenings, they watched the volcano spout flame-colored lava out into the night.

16 MARCH 44

Dearest Mom & Dad,

How are you this March day? It could be windy there in West Texas. I would like to be there to help shovel the sand out of the house.

As for me I am doing alright as usual. I have seen a lot of action since I landed in Italy last Sept. 9. I have been in the line about two thirds of the time—a third in a rest area. I'll probably see plenty more action but I am pretty safe and feel that I have a good chance of boarding that ship for home. Yes, a real good chance so have that fried chicken ready. I received a very nice long letter from Bert. I wrote an article about our first church service in Italy and if the Baptist Standard sees fit they might print it and you will see it or Hubert will maybe. Say hello to everyone and remember me when you pray.

Love,
Cecil

Only people from the South Plains of Texas will understand the reference to shoveling sand out of the house in the spring. Every Eden has its thistles and West Texas farmers say the sandstorms cull the riffraff from the stout-hearted. Perhaps the term "gritty" originated near Roscoe from survivors of their famous spring windstorms.

Something prompted Cecil to be more candid with his parents on how much action he had seen in Italy. The downtime gave him occasion to reflect on what he had endured thus far. Deacon Turner probably assumed it would not alarm his family to mention danger already past. Nevertheless, he carefully ended with an optimistic note and one more reference to homemade fried chicken.

26 MAR 44
Italy

Dearest Dad & Mom,

It's Sunday afternoon and I'm taking it easy. We are getting a little rest again. Maybe by this time you have your home all to yourselves. How do you like your home? No doubt you have read much about the battle of Cassino.

I watched that battle many times from a mountain top while I was with the French.

(mail service is better) I am mailing a package home soon. I will get to send a few things. Maybe I can send everyone something yet. You can explain that I can only send a few at a time. I'll get around to everyone eventually.

I'm well and almost happy. Write to me.

Love,
Cecil

Censors must have informed soldiers when it was safe to mention past engagements. Cecil wrote about battles like Cassino after the fact. Censors evidently would not let him mention the 5th Army to which his division proudly belonged. At first glance of the following letter, the conditioned reader might humorously interpret the X's as "blankety blank," or an expletive usually preceding the word "army." Cecil would have gotten a good laugh at that.

Italy 4/5/44

Dear Dad & Mom,

This Wednesday finds me taking it easy at the Army Rest Center for five days. Regardless of where you are in the XXX army you come back for a 5 day rest about every three months.

I have been shopping some and have sent home a gift for Cassie, Doris, Georgia, etc. I must try to get around to all before I quit.

I have gotten two letters from you fairly recently and I may have some more back at the battery when my 5 day rest is over.

I am doing OK. Always glad to hear from home. Tell everyone hello

Love,
Cecil

Training continued in April near Maddaloni, Italy. These exercises prepared the Division to take part in future operations requiring three types of combat training: basic skills, battalion mountain exercises with supporting artillery, and river crossing maneuvers. Cecil's journal mentions the mountainous village Forino, and the official record shows the command post moved there April 10th. The hilly terrain provided an excellent area for more training exercises.

April 12, 1944

Dear Mom & Dad,   Somewhere in Italy

I have time tonite to let you know I am OK and feeling fine.

I had a snapshot made and am sending it to you. It's not real bad but I ordinarily don't look that slouchy. I think it's about time I wrote you one of those Son to Father letters so real soon I'll write one. Always write a little, Dad, as you do most time.

Love,
Cecil

"On the sun porch of our home near Torino, Italy"

When Cecil left for the service in 1941, his father was actively farming, living on the old home place with his mother. Many changes occurred before the summer of 1944. Cecil's stepmother successfully moved her husband to town then tried to get him to slow down. He heard the same message from his son in the Italian war.

April 13, 1944
Somewhere in Italy

My Dear Dad,

Here is one of those letters especially for you. This Thursday nite finds me doing fine and taking it easy—resting up.

Say, Dad, there is a matter that I would like to discuss. I have been reading between the lines in everybody's letters and have come to the conclusion that you have been working too much and too hard. In the last half dozen letters from you and Mom you have mentioned about always being tired and you haven't written anything in the last few letters. Mom said you were too tired. Someone wrote that you had a broken rib and that you were still working hard. I know you well enough to know that you wouldn't be content if you couldn't work at something, but I thought you had decided to take it easy. When you were living at the old home place and hiring most of the work done you seemed to be getting just the right amount of exercise. I sincerely hope that I am wrong but I have just felt that you have been working too hard.

There is no need of my saying again how much I would like to be at home with you. If I were there I would be just a boy again. I feel like I am still just a kid even though I am 25 and even tho' a fellow told me I looked like I was 30. I would like to be there now and take a walk out across the wheat. Do you still have the combine?

I have hopes of seeing you before many months. Never worry about me but always think and pray for me.

Your son,
Cecil

Some true rest and recreation in Italy, 1944

Cecil with some local boys during rest in Italy, 1944

Cecil with baseball mitt during a rest period in Italy, 1944

4/20/44
Italy

Dear Mom & Dad,

This Thursday nite finds me doing alright and writing you before I go to bed.

I got the Roscoe Times and Sweetwater Reporter today and it had Ava's name in it for playing the piano at the Women's week of prayer.

Veltie told me in his last letter that the two of you were in El Paso and that you were looking strong and healthy now, Dad. I was very glad to hear that you are doing OK Mom.

I am enjoying one of the best relaxation periods that I have ever experienced.

While I was at rest camp I sent a number of gifts to different relatives. If they received and like them I would like you to let me know. I think of you always and like to hear. Pray for me.

Love,
Cecil

The 36th Division knew all the rest and training readied them for a considerable encounter approaching, but no one knew the time or place. Cecil seemed to have all the same questions his family raised at home.

26 April 44
Italy

Dearest Mom & Dad,

This Wednesday finds me doing OK. You have said that you always wanted to hear from me even if there was no news.

There may be a number of things that you wonder about like: How long will the war last? How long will I be overseas after the war with Germany is over? We sometimes think of those things. Someone has said it's all over except the fighting.

You have read how Commando Kelly got such a welcome at Pittsburg. He is the Sgt. York of World War 2. He was in our Division.

You should see twelve men playing volleyball. We have some good players too.

Always remember me when you pray.

Love,
Cecil

American volleyball near Naples, Italy in 1944

In rest area near Torino, Italy 1944

Charles E. "Commando" Kelley was the first American awarded the Congressional Medal of Honor for action on the European continent during World War II. His famous achievements occurred with the 36th Division at Altavista two days following the landing in Italy. Kelley's hometown parade in Pittsburg set a precedent for welcoming returning heroes.

30 April 44
Italy

Dear Mom & Dad,

Tomorrow I go back to the battery after spending ten days in the hospital. I had some kind of an intestinal disorder that caused loose bowels. I felt good all the time and never lost my appetite. The doctor has decided that I was eating something that I was allergic to. We think it may have been tomato juice. I got alright the first day I got to the hospital so these ten days have been a lot of rest for me. I have been reading more the last ten days than I have read for a year. There will probably be a lot of mail for me back at the battery.

I sincerely hope that both of you are having your health and happiness.

It's hard to tell just what's cookin' for us.

The nurses and doctors have been very nice to me. I'll be waiting to hear from you.

Lovingly,
Cecil

"Nothing to do in the rest area near Torino, Italy.
Note the slender horse chestnut trees."

"Radio repair shop trailer, taken during a rest period in Italy,
40 miles from Naples in olive orchard." Cecil on the left.

Working in the radio repair trailer in Italy, Cecil on the left.

Cecil discovered a food allergy to tomatoes while in Italy. The incident prompted a wariness that continued throughout his life. Perhaps this reaction first took place in Italy because so much of their food consists of tomato paste, sauce, and juice.

The 36th Division began moving to a new location in the vicinity of dusty Qualiano before April ended. Days of practice and drills were broken frequently with formal troop reviews and award ceremonies. Meanwhile, headquarters hammered the last minute details into the new offensive.

1 MAY 44
Italy

Dear Veltie, Doris, & Ronny,

I got the Sweetwater Reporter yesterday and the Roscoe Times. It's pretty nice to read up on what happened in the home towns. Hello RONNY

Did the freeze kill barley and oats dead? Is the wheat

coming out? That must have been quite a freeze. Does Dad still have his combine?

I'm sitting out on a hill this afternoon operating a radio in a command car. It's not real important and we'll close it down at nite.

Someone is always getting a package from home with good eats like all sorts of candy, stuffed olives, popcorn, pickles, etc., etc., and other articles like watches, film, pens, etc. You can just, if you want to, gradually start gathering items for me a box. I would like a single edge Gem micromatic razor, some kind of fountain pen and just for a novelty, 4 or 5 cans of sardines. Finish it out with just anything to make it 5 pounds. I hope you get the souvenirs I sent Doris.

Love,
Cecil

5 May 44
Italy

Hello Mom, Dad, & Ava,

This Monday nite finds me back at my battery after being in the hospital for ten days. I feel fine and ready for anything that might come up.

I got three letters today—one from Aunt May, Joy Boles and a nice long one from Roberta. Have you heard from Roberta lately? They are having such wonderful success at their new Church. Aunt May said the article I sent was in the Baptist Standard.

It is pretty here, all the trees are getting green and everything is beginning to grow.

If you ever have a good picture made send me one. I don't even have a picture of you, Mom.

Tell everyone to write me often if they can.
Your Italian son,

Love,
Cecil

His family was finally able to read the article in the *Baptist Standard*. They were all proud of his clear depiction of a church service in the midst of war. Cecil's cousin, Roberta (Bert), was the daughter of Newt's bother, Henry, a Baptist minister. She married a Baptist minister, T. A. Patterson, who became a well-known Baptist leader. Their son, Paige Patterson, continues the Baptist ministry tradition of the family.

A full-scale Allied offensive in Italy began the night of May 11, 1944. Each facet of the scheme tore down the last barriers to Rome. For the opening phase, all available artillery attacked the strong Gustav Line covering Cassino. Cecil's battery plus the three field artillery units of the 36th covered the maneuvers, while a dummy diversion advanced to Qualiano to mislead the enemy. The deception worked, the surprise was complete, and breakthroughs were scored. Although fighting ensued for several more days, by May 17th, the left side of the enemy lines had been breached and success was assured. The 36th artillery units completed their mission and returned to Qualiano to await shipment to Anzio where the second phase was soon to get underway.

13 May 44
Italy

Dearest Dad & Mom,

This after midnight finds me feeling fine and wishing I could see you as usual.

I have enjoyed reading several copies of the Roscoe Times lately.

Italy is pretty and green in spots. There's a lot of fruit trees in bloom and wheat is heading and in the bloom stage. They have a lot of beardless wheat here. You would be surprised to see how small their wheat fields are. Just a few acres and a large percent of it is sown by hand and cut by hand.

Well, Dad, it's nice that you can retire and take it easy but when I get home you will have to be my assistant manager and teach me what I have forgotten.

Before I come home I may study a little, with the Army about gasoline powered motors and their electrical systems.

It hasn't been terribly long since I got your last letters but a little longer than usual.

The Lord bless you and keep you,

Love,
Cecil

In the middle of this offensive push, it is simply amazing he took time to write and maintain the illusion that all was well. After three years of practice, he should be good at it, but it is nonetheless amazing. An entry in Cecil's journal at this date simply states, "Celole—whispering death." Although the meaning is unclear, brief notations such as this would later trigger his memory of this tense period.

14 May 44
Italy

My dear Dad & Mom,

Your letter of May 2 arrived yesterday and was very welcome as it was the first in several days.

I feel bad about the wheat but I remember that some years we made very little. I always liked growing wheat.

I have just returned from a service we had honoring our mothers. The new chaplain there was a Southern Baptist from North Carolina.

I'm glad you liked the little article in the Baptist Standard. Aunt May happened to see it too.

Won't you breathe an extra prayer for me now and then. I know that you are praying for me and I also mention you when I pray. I believe the Lord pays special attention to prayers from foxholes.

Your letters mean a lot to me. Don't forget to always write a little, Dad. Sometimes a long letter.

Love,
Cecil

His reminders to pray were more insistent and consistent during dangerous periods. "Foxhole prayers" can encompass turning to God in any crisis, whether in a war zone or a hospital emergency room. Many writers have considered the aspects of these desperate conversations with their Maker. Cecil not only considered them valid, but believed God gave special consideration to urgent prayers as any father hearing his child's cry for help.

"Going to Anzio, (carriers) Etter and Swope"

The 36th Division sailed from Pazzuoli near Naples beginning on May 18, 1944. The Division was put ashore at the Anzio perimeter on May 22 and was immediately involved in holding actions. The Texans followed up through Cisterna and entered the line of the approach to Rome by way of Velletri. Cecil made notes in his journal concerning a wine cellar and a "hot command post" during this time period.

Most of Cecil's letters ended with a reminder to pray for him but in May of 1944 he took the urgency one step further. Over the past few days he was in a position to find a deep appreciation for sandbags and foxholes.

The Bible tells us, "The effective fervent prayer of a righteous man avails much" (James 5:16, NKJV). Cecil knew his father was a righteous man and a prayer from him could mean the difference in life and death.

24 May 44

My Dear Mom & Dad,

Day before yesterday I received a very nice box of candy from Ava. It has not been so very long since I had a letter from you and I got two Roscoe Times yesterday.

I also had a letter from Veltie and from what he says there will be very little or no wheat cut. That even discourages me a little as far away as I am. There is usually good that follows all bad crops.

The longer I stay overseas the more I want to go home but my morale is still up enough to sweat out the rest of this war. The longer I stay overseas the more convinced I am that sand bags and foxholes are a guy's best friends. You can bet your boots that I have breathed a prayer from my trench or fox-hole.

Things must be pretty there at your new home. I bet you have the prettiest flowers in town. I always marveled how industrious and active you are, Mom. You know some people think they are old at sixty. Please don't work too hard though, and, Dad, you would probably write every day if you knew how much a letter means. Remember a prayer may bring me home safe.

Love,
Cecil

The push to Rome had one major obstacle—the enemy stronghold of Velletri. The Germans severely punished other efforts to climb the sharp hills leading up to the village. In late May, two regiments had pulled back from their frontal assault, had circled around the town, and climbed the two thousand foot height behind Velletri before the Germans were aware. By the end of the next day, Velletri had fallen in a risky but successful plan. Having learned from the disastrous frontal assault at the Rapido River, Velletri was a huge success that paved the way to Rome, which was lying defenseless in the Army's path.

During most of May, the clashes and snipers were many and the soldiers had to dig deep pits and live like moles to avoid the German fire. These foxholes offered safety, but were damp and hard on the human body. The most amusing visual image Cecil relayed about his exploits during the war came from trying to dress up one of these accommodations during some respite between assaults.

June 3, 44
Somewhere in Italy

My Dear Mom & Dad,

Tonite I am doing OK. I have a nasty cold but most people can fight off a cold. I think I got mine sleeping underground so much.

A letter came yesterday stating you have mailed me some candy. I'm sure it will be here soon. Thank you very much! Aunt Ina and her family sent me a box of things that never arrived.

There is a lot of fruit here most of which isn't ripe yet. The other day I stumbled into a cherry tree loaded and ripe. The funny part–after I stripped the tree I wasn't even sick.

I had the privilege of seeing American Anti-aircraft shoot a Nazi bomber out of the sky. It went down like a rocket.

One of the things that would amuse me if I were a civilian back home is the electric lights we rigged up in our dugout once. When the line wasn't moving very fast three of us dug in like a bunch of gophers. Headquarters has a jeep motor which powers a generator so I ran a line to it and put in a socket. Electric lights in fox holes–some class!

Here's hoping it has rained since I last heard from you. It's funny how rain affects the lives of so many people.

Mom, I wish you could see all the roses here. Red, white, orange, yellow, and pink roses. There are as many in one city block here as there are in the city of Roscoe.

Don't know if I will be home for Xmas or not but if I am, save me some "white" meat off the turkey.

There's not much to write about. The war goes on and each day brings victory nearer.

You are so close now you can walk to Church. How is the Church? Say hello to Bro. Elrod for me.

May the Lord bless and be ever near to you. Always remember–

Love,
Cecil

"Each day brings victory nearer" was a new optimism that was catching on as the Allies had the Germans on the run. It was the 36th Division sneak play, conceived and executed by Major General Fred L. Walker and his staff that broke the German line at Velletri and opened the race track to Rome. The Germans were on the run and the 36th was taking ground as fast as they could march. Cecil made a note in his journal about staying just outside Rome on movie lots on June 3rd. Throughout the morning of June 5th, the troops moved through the eternal city's tumultuous welcome and isolated German snipers. Beside the word "Rome" in Cecil's journal is the understatement: "The Welcome." He described later the spontaneous parade to cheer the Texans' arrival. The historic significance of this event could not escape even these exhausted soldiers but there was no time for sightseeing or writing home, as utmost speed was necessary to keep in contact with the fleeing Germans. [16]

10 JUNE 44

Dearest Mom & Dad,

In the history books for the next several hundred years you will find the answer to why I haven't written more often lately.

I am OK, well, and happy.

Love,
Cecil

Although terribly tired by constant chase and sleepless nights, the men's morale was kept high by the taste of the greatest victory since they crushed the Germans at Salerno. Casualties were extremely light, due to skillful employment of tanks and infantry artillery which gave the Nazis no rest. So fast did our men move that the command post went ahead four times in one day.[17]

The Division continued its rampage up the Italian peninsula. Troops discovered supplies and rations tossed aside, confirming the Germans' quick retreat. Cecil made a humorous note that they had "kraut to eat—by Civitavecchia." Soldiers had several slang terms for the Germans, including the well-earned dietary nickname, "Krauts." He also mentioned two friends in his notes during this time—"Foster captured, McIntyre killed."

The Texans met with sporadic resistance as Germans vainly attempted to delay the Americans. The city of Piombino marked the goal of the 29-day advance which had covered 240 miles and had netted 5,000 enemy prisoners.[18]

While the 36th completed the liberation of Italy, they were encouraged to hear of the invasion of western France. To those just hitting the beaches, the war was just beginning. However, with more Allied troops in Europe, the Texans felt the war entering a stage where the end might be in sight.

12 JUNE 44
Italy

Dearest Mom & Dad,

The two boxes of candy arrived today and Boy! Were they good. Maybe I should say Boy! are they good for I will make them last a day or two. The box was in good shape and the candy is very good. Thanks a million! It seems funny that a fellow should crave things like that but I have seen men above 30 who would have given five dollars for a chocolate bar.

Needless to say I'm doing fine and still operating radios. I think we are playing an important role in this divisions fighting now. Some day I will explain in detail our part.

Let me express again how much I love to hear from home. Both of you take care of yourselves and I will mow the lawn when I get home. Tell Veltie I had the laugh of my life. We stumbled into a boxcar load of burning "Kraut." Two gallon cans were strewn everywhere.

Love,
Cecil

Two weeks after the 36th drove the Germans out of Rome, Cecil is finally at liberty to discuss it in his letters. The overwhelming reception was something this farm boy from Roscoe had never seen and must have been a huge adrenalin rush for all the troops as the red carpet was hurriedly unfurled for these racing Americans.

18 JUNE '44

Dear Mom & Dad,   Italy

I wish you could have been with us when we went marching down the streets of Rome. It was at the crack of dawn. The people almost ate us up alive they were so glad to see the exit of the Germans and the entrance of the Americans. About five cute girls almost climbed up into my vehicle where I was operating a radio. I wished I could have taken them along. We stopped for some time in Rome and talked to the people. We talked to one girl who spoke English very well and had lived in America at one time.

Yes, the Fifth Army finally put the Krauts on the run and

they haven't stopped exactly yet. This is the condition I have waited a long time to see the Krauts in. They haven't had time to destroy food and ammunition that they left behind. I have eaten delicious "Kraut," cherries, cookies, sardines, sugar, cheese, etc. at Jerry's expense. I am doing fine. Hope to see you soon. Don't work too hard.

Love,
Cecil

Once the Northern area was more secure, the soldiers were given passes to visit Rome. In one of these visits, Cecil had a photo taken to send home. He also enjoyed the Italian people in the area and, of course, enjoyed the countryside and farmers.

Quick Photo to send home

Written by his friend Bill Hutchins, "The most fraternizing picture I ever saw! Sgt. Turner caught in the act!"   The troops were encouraged not to "fraternize" with the locals.

22 JUNE 44
Somewhere in Italy

My Dear Mom & Dad,

I received a letter from you yesterday and you were anxious to hear from me since the fall of Rome. I have written several times since we took Rome. Naturally I'm OK.

I like north Italy much better than the Naples area. I have some of the cutest little Italian girlfriends!

There is no news much from here.

You must be anxious about the other front. Everyone else is I guess.

I am so sleepy I can hardly finish this letter
Excuse me

Remember I'm OK.

All my love,
Cecil

29 JUNE 44

Dearest Mom & Dad,

I received your letter of June 14 today and it seems that some of my letters do not make it since you said you had not heard from me since about 4 weeks. I haven't been writing as much lately but I have been writing every few days.

I have mentioned my getting two boxes of candy from home. One I believe Ava and Bennie sent. The other was a box of candy with nuts and box of chocolates all in the same package. All three boxes were very nice and so good. Thank you very much! I'll get the one from Veltie maybe soon.

I liked the country north of Rome a lot more than the area around Naples. Your air mail letter came yesterday with the account of the wreck. I am so glad neither of you were hurt. If you don't be more careful I'll get mad and come home before the job is finished.

That's all for now. I'll try to write more often now.

Lots of love and best wishes to you both.

I'm yours,
Cecil

Before their invasion of Southern France, the 36th enjoyed some much needed rest near the location of their Italian invasion almost a year earlier. It must have seemed strange to be swimming and relaxing on Salerno beach where many friends had lost their lives. There on the sand that had witnessed their battle baptism, the Texans paraded in farewell to General Walker. Major General Dahlquist took command as the 36th prepared for its second invasion.

"Salerno Beach—Italy. That's me alright—looks like Hubert!"

"USO Show in Italy, M.C. on GI truck"

4 JULY 44
Somewhere in Italy

My Dear Dad & Mom,

This finds me resting up at the rest Camp. I will be here five days. There have been some good movies here.

I have waited some thirty minutes trying to think what to write. There is never anything to write except that I am OK—would like to be at home. I have been in combat 178 days since last Sept. 9.

I could write about church services but we haven't had any lately. I have said everything that I can think of about the Italian people in my other letters. I do like Northern Italy better.

I must write again soon. Always remember me in your prayers.

Love,
Cecil

In the letters to follow, when no church services are mentioned, we can assume that the chaplains were too busy with other duties. It is unfortunate that the opportunity to worship together did not occur when the men needed it most.

Cecil notes in his journal they had returned to Paestum and could "see old spots." He also mentioned having "ice cream, too!" Throughout his life, the superiority of that frozen dessert was faithfully declared. Perhaps enhanced by the circumstances or years, Italian ice cream made an impressive memory.

Following their relaxed weeks on the coast, the Division would spend their last days in Italy getting equipment and men ready to move the war into Southern France.

"Myself and Sgt. Robert Meyer of San Antonio, Ten miles out of Naples—Mobile Radio Station"

"Giving no. 13 an overhaul in preparation for the invasion of S. France"

"Taking it easy, ten miles out of Naples a few weeks before the invasion of Southern France."

17 JULY 44
Italy

Dearest Mom & Dad,

This Monday afternoon finds me OK.
I was sorry to hear that you mashed your thumb. I remember that cuts and bruises were always slow to heal on your hands, and mine have been a lot the same way here in Italy.

I had a letter from Veltie too and he said the wheat made about 6–7 bu.–better than nothing. What is the price?

Things are OK with me. I see a show about every other nite and now and then we have ice cream. Thanks to our quartermaster we have enough ingredients to make cream and let some Italian freeze it.

I had a nice letter from the pastor at Merkel. He read the article in the Baptist Standard and said he was going to send me the Merkel newspaper if I wasn't already getting it. I can hardly wait to visit the Merkel Church again.

All my love,
Cecil

The short time Cecil was in Merkel running the grocery store, he enjoyed the church and pastor there. What a surprise it was for that preacher to see an article in the Baptist state newspaper written by that young, curly-headed butcher.

July 31, 1944
Somewhere in Italy

My Dear Dad & Mom,

I am feeling fine this afternoon and not doing a thing. I got this money order today and I will enclose it. You may deposit it for me and if you find it convenient see what my total is now.

I got a nice letter yesterday from Ava and a picture today of her and H.C. Tell her I got it. I wrote her before I got the picture.

Also, I got a very nice letter from Irene and pictures of all her kids. She certainly has a nice family now. Mo Wheeler wrote me the other day.

Mozelle wrote me a letter the other day. She gave me a

description of a Sunday Morning Service at the church and she said you were in your pew, Dad.

Ava said you got the picture I sent you that I had made in Rome.

Always eager to hear from both of you. Be sweet and careful

Lovingly,
Cecil

First Baptist Church, Roscoe, Texas resembled many churches then and still today. Regular attendees have a designated pew. No official nameplate is affixed or written proclamation to that effect, but acknowledgement comes by time spent anchoring the church in a certain location. As creatures of habit we migrate to the known and comfortable. It gave Cecil comfort to have friends mention seeing his father in the usual location. The world was not completely turned upside down if Newt Turner was in his pew on Sunday.

Studio picture of Ava and Clay Boston

August 5, 1944
Italy

Dearest Mom & Dad,

I don't know but I but I think this is Sunday. I would have to call someone over here to find out–someone with a calendar. It's a hot sunny day and I'm sitting around in the shade of the apple trees taking it easy. Mail service is good now. I got a letter from a girl in Mass. in five days.

Nothing ever happens to me now. There's no news at all to write. You must be doing pretty good, Dad, I see in the papers about the shortage of farm implements and you buy a new three row.

We sure do have a good Battery commander now. He is from Abilene. There's not many as good as he is. He taught school at Abilene High School and was at McMurry for about five years. He is Captain Hiner and he just has our battery of about 96 men.

I'll mention again the nice picture I got of Ava & Clay.

I have a birthday the 13th. I will be better than a quarter of a century old–26. Pardon me while I see if my hair is graying. Ask the Lord to be with us until Jerry is finished.

Love,
Cecil

Cecil rarely mentioned the officers of his Division over the years he was in the military. Among his souvenirs of the war, however, was a post-war newspaper clipping from the Abilene paper. He had saved an article about Lt. Col. Vaiden P. Hiner from Abilene who was later involved with training for the Korean Conflict. Cecil was impressed by this man and continued to follow his career.

Italy

My dear Dad & Mom,

This night finds me Corporal of the guard and I come off in a few minutes. Here's a line or two to let you know I'm OK. I'm doing swell.

I had a laugh when someone wrote that the reason they hadn't written before they thought I was coming home soon. Don't look for me home until the war is much nearer over than it is now. I never did tell you about how they send 1% of the fellows home each month. There is always someone who needs to go more than I. Maybe their nerves are shot, they are older, married, etc.

How is everything at home? Let me know when anything new happens.

Here's a picture I had made for you.

Love,
Cecil

Eleven months of Italian warfare had changed the Texas Division. The ranks of the National Guardsmen slowly had been thinned. Of 11,000 casualties (dead and wounded), 2,000 were Texans; at Salerno alone: 1,900 casualties, 750 from Texas. But the 36th had made the Germans pay heavily, too—6,000 prisoners in addition to enormous numbers killed and wounded.[19]

Cecil played a part in the successful Italian campaign but knew it was just the first step in the long struggle ahead. The letters did not hint that soon he would be writing from a different country as they continued to push toward the birthplace of Nazism.

CHAPTER 4

★ ★ ★ ★ ★

France

Now faith is the substance of things hoped for,
the evidence of things not seen.

Hebrews 11:1 (NKJV)

The Allied Command had long contemplated invading the French Riviera.

First proposed in December of 1943, the original plan was a coordinated double jab at both Northern and Southern France. Postponement of the attack became necessary when the grueling Italian Campaign lingered. During the early summer of 1944, the Allies proposed an August date for the Riviera landing. Not until June 24th, however, did they nominate the Texas Division for the project and pulled them away from the Italian front for a rushed program of invasion training on the beaches of Salerno. The 36th Division was under command of the U. S. 5th Army during all of its service in Italy, September 9, 1943 through August, 1944. It was assigned to the U. S. 7th Army in the invasion of Southern France and thereafter, August, 1944 through the end of war.

The Germans were well aware of the logical target in Southern France. However, in late July, the Normandy invasion was now advancing and the onrushing drive to Paris would follow. The enemy defenses of the southern coastal areas were being reduced to meet the serious breaches in the north. The Pictorial History of the 36th

"Texas" Infantry Division records:

> Our intelligence determined that the German Nine-teenth Army, soon to oppose the (southern) Allied invasion, had been streamlined from 13 to 9 divisions—still, however, an effective force if it could be concentrated. With the Lufwaffe weakened and the German Navy, never top notch, practically eliminated, our forces, strong in these departments, entered the operation with confidence.[1]

The Texans were put through a mock invasion of Gaeta Bay, Italy just days before the French invasion. The dress rehearsal, appropriately named "Cowpuncher II," was not completely successful but the troops were again bivouacked in the vicinity of Qualiano for operation "Anvil." On Cecil's birthday, August 13th, 1,000 ships left Italy with the Seventh Army's mighty armada of men and equipment and swung between the islands of Corsica and Sardinia before heading for San Raphael. Unlike the fairly smooth voyages from New York and North Africa, Cecil's trip in the cramped hot landing craft across the Mediterranean to Southern France was gut-wrenching.

Cooperation with the French had helped to clear 50,000 civilians from the four beach targets designated: Red, Yellow, Green, and Blue. None of the areas were without hazards—underwater obstacles, concrete pillboxes, gun emplacements, stone sea walls, submarine mine netting, and of course, all of this was flanked by extensive firepower.

On the morning of August 15, the Texans began their beach approach under a cover of rocket barrages and overwhelming naval and aerial bombardment. Effective contingency plans supported the successful landing of all forces, even when Red Beach, the main avenue of attack, was unable to be cleared of mines. The official records use the term "light opposition" for the morning and Cecil wrote in his notes, "San Raphael, easy landing, bomb missed me."

By D-Day plus one, all the beaches were secure and positions inland were consolidated against sporadic enemy opposition. The 36th had made contact with a group of French commandos late on the second day. It was estimated there were 45,000 partially armed Frenchmen in the area with sabotage material to assist in the Allied plans. This relationship with the regular French Army and the rural guerrilla Maquis would continue until the Division left France. This allied force seized a German camp and cleared the town of Frejus without opposition. Cecil was impressed by a winery at Frejus and included an entry in his journal.

At the end of the second day, the 36th was mopping up the capture of San Raphael and had rounded up 900 prisoners of war. The Texans advanced 100 miles in one day after the landing and would proceed 200 miles from the beaches within the first week. In his notes, Cecil mentioned the city of "Draguinan—on a hill" where the befuddled Commander of the German 62nd Corps was nabbed along with his entire staff. In appreciation of the liberation of the city, the Texans were given a gift.

> [T]he mayor of Draguinan came to a 36th Division officer and said, 'I know what you want.' Then he led the colonel to a beautiful, walled garden, quiet and shaded. 'You want a cemetery. All the people of my town have contributed to give you this land. It is the gift of the people of Draguinan to their liberators.' [2]

The liberated French, an imaginative and vivacious race, seemed more sincere than the Italians in their appreciation. They tossed flowers and fruit at jeeps and many of them repeated their gratitude over and over again. The same enthusiasm unfolded as they cursed the German prisoners forced to march through the streets. A monument at the beach near San Raphael was soon erected which can still be read today:

> Over this defended beach the men of the 36th U. S. Infantry Division stormed ashore 15 August 1944, together with the French allies. They began here the drive that took them across France, through Germany and into Austria to the final destruction of the German Armies and the Nazi regime.[3]

After the operation, Allied Headquarters boasted of the Riviera Invasion: "A model of effective organization, cooperation of all services, and vigor of action—one of the best coordinated efforts in all military history."[4]

Deacon Turner's family had waited several weeks before a letter finally arrived and consoled their fears. During the span of the French invasion, Cecil's duties required every moment and prevented him from writing. By the time he managed an opportunity to scribble a note home, Turner was a year older and could proudly announce their latest conquest.

Aug 21, 1944
France

Dearest Mom & Dad,

This evening finds me feeling fine and thinking about home and everyone I love. It gives me great pleasure to inform you that I am in Southern France. Last Sept. 9, I landed on D day in Italy and I came in on D day this time in the invasion of France. I came over in a XXX craft made to carry about XXX. I was the fellow who thought I would never be seasick. I was wrong, so sick the first day at sea I didn't care whether the ship sank or just burned. I got some seasick pills though the next day and felt good as new. I will also be able to tell my grandchildren that we touched off Corsica and I went ashore. The story you have heard about the corruption and the low morals of the French so far are untrue. So far, I like the French very much and I think France and the U.S. can be great friends. Maybe I should say that I have seen some of the prettiest women ever in France. They are very nice and insist on planting a kiss on both your cheeks when we occupy their country. I will write again later tonite. We are already eating well.

Hello to all.

All my love,
Cecil

On the same day as the next letter, part of the 36th Division entered Grenoble, a lovely university city nestled in the French Alps. "Welcome" shouted the front page of the town's newspaper, and continued:

Yesterday without warning, we saw them rising up at the far end of [town] . . . those well-built boys in khaki, those strong, calm fellows who in 1918 shared with [us] all the sufferings of battle, all the joys of victory.

At first no one dared to believe it. The Americans? They are here? Already? At last astride their funny little jeeps, perched high on their heels, reminding one of the far west . . . The wildly enthusiastic crowd, which shouted its welcome to the liberating troops . . . found fresh voices to shout an enthusiastic welcome to the big attractive giants. Welcome to you all! You who have come from the distant provinces if Illinois, Ohio, Alabama, or Texas . . . you all who have come to help France get rid of a nightmare which has lasted four interminable years, and to aid her to rediscover her true soul.[5]

August 22
Southern France

Dearest Mom & Dad,

This is my second French letter. You will probably get them both the same day so I will continue the same subjects. Incidentally I'm well, happy, healthy, whole, fat, mean, etc.

Coming on the beach on D-day I had my radio station set up in less than thirty minutes after I came ashore and contacted two or three other stations in my network. The French are really fighting too. They fight with whatever they can get (Bless 'em). Those 8 ½ words I learned in Italy working with the French Army kinda come in handy. The French in a town we moved through showered us with tomatoes, apples, pears, etc. I mentioned how cute the French girls are. Now I know why the boys brought back a few for wives after the last war.

It's getting dark so I must stop. I had another experience after which I didn't know whether to thank the Lord for protecting me or thank the Nazi workers for sabotage in munition plants.

I'll write again soon. Love,
Cecil

Cecil on the left with a new French friend and army buddy.

Cecil with a French girlfriend he met in Southern France.

Cecil's journal discloses an incident at Marsanne — "shelled out 100,000,000 mm," plus the note, "scared stiff." Once again, Deacon Turner escaped from a dud that could have claimed his life. Through this period, fighting continued to be sporadic. The front was advancing rapidly to keep in close contact with the Nazis on the run. In their haste, pockets of undiscovered Germans were left behind the line to be dealt with by troops in the rear. It was a dangerous situation, but to keep up the pace, (as much as 90 miles in one 14 hour period), every motorized vehicle was loaded with troops.

In the following letter, Cecil filled in details to his family as to his responsibilities in the war. In his box of memoirs, Cecil saved some notes made during those hours on the radio coordinating artillery support. Most of the cryptic messages are lost on the civilian reader but a few give some clue as to the importance of those long vigilant nights wearing headphones. Six number blocks, such as 000–000, were artillery map coordinates to tell the location of points of interest or targets. The three digit codes were radio contacts with artillery units such as the 131st or 155th, under control of Division Artillery. The four number blocks are recognizable as military time notes using the military 24 hour clock — 1617 is 17 minutes after four in the afternoon. "Fired Ruby" may refer to a preplanned artillery barrage fired at a certain location, elevation, and number of rounds.

FROM A'SA	2 EXPL.	975-343	FLAME & BLACK SMOKE	
J3A to us	town	084-345	dive bombing	1617
N11	1 or 2 ENERGUNS	043-318		1625

FIRED RUBY WITH GOOD EFFECT. POSSIBLY 1 DIRECT HIT

J3A to 131	personnel at	043-290	blowing down trees	1707
	bridge			
		024-332	impassible	1710
		985-317	3 tanks friendly	1710
		052-272	road block	1711

J3A to 155 3 horse drawn arty. approaching cross road

at 989-302 at about 100 yd. intervals   1800

The Germans still widely utilized antiquated, horse-drawn artillery. It was a sad discovery by the 36th while chasing the enemy in Northern Italy, to find the Germans had slaughtered hundreds of horses to prevent them from falling into the hands of the Allies.

Aug 27, 1944
Southern France

My dear Mom & Dad,

Go across the street and say hello to Ava

Once again, I find that I have waited several days before I had a chance to write, even to you. I don't think you will mind tho' when I tell you that I have been so busy dealing, or helping deal the enemy a hard blow. Right now, I am on the radio as net control. Any minute I might receive a message that an observer had spotted some tanks in a little wooded area and asks if we can fire on them. Then we would know where the area was on the map and could tear them to bits with artillery. The observer might come back with "there goes one up in flames now." That is a hasty and crude illustration but you get it I'm sure.

I have a good place to stay here with some French people. They are country people and I like them a lot. I like to tell them about our farms and machinery. They have some made by McCormick and Deering. I can help them and they can help me. I don't remember whether I told you about spending my birthday at sea or not–off the coast of Corsica. Coney said my birthday was the 14th. I thought it was the 13th. Maybe she is right.

I got mail the other day but none from home. A letter from Maxie, Betty Jowell, & Coney. Good luck! I love you,

Cecil

      Coming from a large family and a small town was an advantage during mail call. Turner's niece, Maxie, and sister, Coney, kept him informed of home. While friends in town kept him aware of other news.

      Cecil was meeting many French locals during this time. They gladly housed many of the troops, especially those attached to the headquarters unit that did not travel as much as most units. Cecil's journal mentions "my French girl" at Marsanne and another "girl gives me her picture—brother in FFI [French Forces of the Interior] at St. Germaine Du-Bois." Over the next few months he met several valiant members of the French underground, including a woman who was a leader of the Free French movement.

Cecil with "woman who was head of the Free French movement and her daughter"

Cecil operating his radio from inside a French home.

The same day as the previous letter, the official report recorded a comment about the work of the Division Artillery. A three-pronged attack was planned on the German stronghold at Montelimar. The infantry reported heavy resistance in an outlying area, but withdrew to accommodate artillery concentrations on the town. Four enemy tanks and several big guns were taken out. "Division Artillery Air Ops reported enemy vehicles jamming the road in attempt to ford the Drome River. Artillery fire exacted a heavy toll."[6]

Many consider the Battle of Montelimar one of the greatest for the Texans during this phase of the war. As Velletri had been the "cork in the bottle" to Rome, the Germans began to put pressure on the 36th at Montelimar. Enemy strength was at least double the Allies. However, considerable artillery reinforced the 36th who was soon joined by one of the combat teams from the 45th Division. Elements of three German Divisions began pounding the lines of the Texas Division. These included the best unit Hitler had in Southern France, the 11th Panzer Division. The battle lasted over a week with our troops forced to withdraw several times.

It was the artillery at Montelimar that counted most and swayed the tide of the battle. During the eight days Division field artillery battalions fired over 37,000 rounds at the confined, retreating army. Supporting fires from an attached battalion brought the total number of rounds expended to considerably more than 75,000.[7]

For most of the 36th Division's service in Europe, it fought alongside the 45th Division (former Oklahoma National Guard) and the 3rd Division (regular Army—Audie Murphy's unit). All three divisions were in Southern France in August of 1944 and all collaborated in closing the gap at Montelimar, trapping the German 19th Army. The loss to the enemy was enormous—11,000 casualties (dead and wounded), 2,100 vehicles lost, 1,500 horses perished, and the big guns of 3 divisions virtually destroyed. By the end of August, the Battle of Montelimar was over and the new drive north began.

In early September the new phase was best described by an officer's diary entry, "Looks like our CP (command post) will move up Highway 7 tomorrow. Race starts again!"[8] With enemy resistance light and invaluable assistance by the French Maquis, the T-Patchers bounced along on every available vehicle for long rides through scenic countryside. They enjoyed ideal weather as the French gratefully welcomed their liberators. Days passed without any sight of the enemy. Most resistance was light; only once did the Germans turn, and attempt to make a stand. This period brought fast gains and rich rewards. Most of Southern France had been freed and the Nazis were falling back in disorder. The southern attack had been an overwhelming success.

September 7, 1944
France
To Ava–Candy Received–

Dearest mom & Dad, & Ava,

This rainy day finds me doing OK and not quite as busy as I usually am. I still have nice experiences with the French people. Yesterday there were four of us who ate dinner with a lady whose husband is a prisoner in Germany. She had two cute little girls one five and an eight year old. She was so glad to see us! We are sometimes the first American soldiers in these places and we sure get a welcome. You should see the people line the road when they hear the Americans are coming. They rush out to give us fruit, eggs, bread, etc. I saw a terrible thing the other day–day before yesterday. There were a number of pretty country homes along the road close together and the Krauts had burned 12 of them. The people were out cheering us and their homes were still burning. They sure have a lot of courage.

We are close enough to Switzerland that I see a lot of wooden shoes and funny dresses. I feel pretty good about the war now. It can't last too long in Europe. Always remember me when you pray. Say hello to all.

Lovingly,
Cecil

The Americans were surprised at the strong influence the Swiss had on southern and eastern France. The villagers despised the Germans and many worked or cooperated with the French underground movement. As much as they hated Nazis, they adored the Allies. The liberators welcomed the wine and cheese lavished on them but also gained a mistaken impression of the ease in defeating Hitler's forces. In Cecil's notes on September 8, 1944, he mentions "Besancon—School—people eat us up and our candy too." No wonder Cecil and all the troops thought the war would end soon if the Nazis were this easy to chase out of Europe.

One of the daughters of the grateful French that housed
Cecil during his months in France.

September 13, 1944
Somewhere in France

Dearest Mom & Dad,

*I'll bet you don't very often write me at 3:30 in the
morning—well that's what I'm doing right now. I guess
the whole world isn't as busy in the dead of night even
France seems to sleep when it gets that late. The radio is
making a lot of noise. But there are no messages right now
so here's a letter for you. That gives you a general idea of
what your youngest son is doing right now in France.*

*My last letter was from Irene. She had enjoyed the visit of
you two very much.*

—A small box of candy from a girl I have seen only once in Florida. Some people are so very thoughtful.

I haven't been homesick in France except one day we were set up in an International Harvester implement warehouse and I mowed some grass with a lawn mower. That reminded me of home too much! I suppose this is enough of nonsense from me especially at this hour in the morning. I'll be home when I catch up–HA!

Hello AVA!

Love,
Cecil

With the war going well there was much to see in France and little time to think of home—except when Cecil had the opportunity to play with some farm equipment. The smell and feel of the mower took him across the ocean to Nolan County. His family would have enjoyed a photo of him driving an International implement in France.

The success of the march through France would continue through most of September, but not without firefights, including some that were severe. Unlike the free movement through Maquis territory in southern France, almost every day one regiment or the other encountered the enemy. But the 36th drove on, reaching the Moselle River at Remiremont on September 20, 1944.[9]

Sept 17, 1944
Somewhere in France

Hello there!

Here it is in the wee hours of the morning again and as I must stay awake anyways I'll write the note to let you know I'm still as safe and sound as ever. I'm surprised that all of you didn't know where I was on Sept 1ˢᵗ, the postmark on your last letter which I received yesterday. The radio and the New York Times announced that the 6ᵗʰ Division invaded France the next day after we landed. Thanks very much for the picture—now I have one of you both.

There's not much to write. We are just pushing the Krauts out of France and the French people still give us a big Welcome. You should have seen one of the fellows frying potatoes and me frying eggs—all a gift from the people.

I'm thinking of raising my allotment from $40 to $70. It's nice to hear that everything is OK at home and everyone is well. Say hello to everyone for me.

Love,
Cecil

Newt and Martha Turner in front of their house in Roscoe, Texas.

Even though news of the invasion was quick to hit the headlines in the major cities, busy farm families had little opportunity or time to search for the latest news. With so many fronts being covered, it must have been hard at times to follow exactly where the 36th was located.

The Allies continued to enjoy gifts from the grateful French as they pushed north. They were freed from the hated Germans, or "Boche" as they referred to them.

Hurried, homemade American flags flew in honor of their liberators. Traveling to new locations was no small task, more because of the enthusiasm of the freed French than from the actions of the enemy. They were besieged at times with food and wine.

Sept 20, 1944
Somewhere in France

Dearest Mom & Dad,

Just a few words again in the dead of the night. I'm healthy and doing OK. I'm going to mail a pair of wooden shoes home today. You may enjoy showing them to your friends and someday I can show them. If they don't get in the way too much keep them for me.

Keep Writing.

Lovingly,
Cecil

The wooden shoes did make it home and were quite the conversation piece. As the 36th moved north, they came closer to the Swiss border and made a stop at Luxeuil where many soldiers had the luxury of a warm bath in their hot sulfur spas. The 36th planned to cross the Moselle River as the respite and good weather ended. About the fast-paced tour of Northern France one T-Patcher stated:

Mostly we remember the good things about those days from Montelimar to the Moselle. If Jerry had any artillery he was moving too fast to use it. The French people were fine genuine people who welcomed us into their homes whenever we had a moment to stop. If there weren't as many flags and flowers as there had been in Southern France, there was just as wholesome a kind of people that reminded us of the folks back home in Texas and Ohio.

One thing about the people of France was that the welcome was in direct proportion to the amount of artillery we had to use to drive the Germans out of their towns. Later, in the Vosges, where a lot of us fought our hearts out to take a town, we found a cold and icy attitude among the people.

It perhaps is worthy of note that, also, the people in the Vosges, and the Rhine Valley, were often Germanic in ethnic origin, so the attitudes might reflect a leaning toward the Germans. In Southern France, a Frenchman could hardly speak the word "Boche" without spitting.[10]

The first pursuit from the beach landing in France had ended in the great battle of Montelimar. The second pursuit slowed down from a chase to the bitter, but short-lived battle to cross the Moselle River. It was there that the enemy chose to begin their most serious effort at stopping the American onslaught, which was the prelude to a long, cold winter of inch-by-inch battle.[11]

Sept. 21, 1944
Somewhere in France

My dear Dad,

Yesterday I received a letter with nearly a half page you had written so I decided it was time for another one of those father and son letters. I enjoyed the last letter as I do all of them.

I suppose you were joking when you said I could bring one of these French girls home with me but even though you probably were it's not as bad an idea as some people think. There are many reasons why I will wait until I get back and find an American girl. A number of the French girls speak a little English. They are very nice people but they are quite different from we Americans. I will send a picture of one maybe soon.

Dad, I am enclosing a copy of the commendation given to me for fighting in Italy when we were against Cassino. You remember when I wrote you last winter about doing liaison work with the French. I would sure hate to go through all of that again.

I haven't mentioned it but I am a sergeant now. I was still a corporal when the citation was written.

Wish you would keep this for me. We will show it to my grandchildren. (if any)

This is about all for tonite I guess, Dad; I get to sleep in a few minutes as I will turn the radio over to someone else. We will try not to let Hitler get away like you said.

Your letters are always a lot of courage.

God bless my Dad!

Love,
Cecil

P.S. Wish you would thank mom for writing to me faithfully. She is very kind. C.T.

The Army promoted Cecil to sergeant some time earlier but he was never quite comfortable with all the military trappings. His desired promotion did not involve stripes, but the straps of civilian farm overalls. Nevertheless, he did want his grandchildren to see the citation one day. Deacon Turner believed in what they were doing in Europe and would not let Hitler get away. His father's letters kept his spirit up and courage strong, but Sergeant Turner still longed for lengthy conversations with his dad.

Early the morning of September 20, 1944, the first troops crossed the Moselle River. It was not really that much of an obstacle but they needed a guide. No one could be found until the 90-year old Mayor of Rayon appeared. He had the agility of a youth and knew the way through the trackless forest. After making the trip alone to the edge of the Moselle, he returned to lead the Americans across. [12] The first T-Patchers waded through waist deep water to secure the first bridgehead. This, however, was not to be the case for the units to follow.

The Germans were much more prepared further up and down the river as more crossings were attempted. The enemy was desperate in their efforts to hold it. At Remiremont, where the German's sole escape route over the last intact bridge across the Moselle lay, a stubborn enemy dug in his heels. The Nazis were in a favorable position and had boasted they would hold their defenses all winter behind their water barrier. The security of a bridgehead was threatened when enemy infiltrations and fresh German strength continued to flare up. To make matters worse, rain lasting for several days combined with autumn cold imposed a bitter hardship on the attacking Texans. Similar to the terrain in Italy, there were few places of shelter in these scrubby highlands. Extreme exposure and fatigue caused more casualties than battle and reduced fighting strength to a nub.[13]

Cecil did not mail a letter during these difficult two weeks. The bloody Moselle River was a costly battlefield for the 36th. Among the many casualties was a wounded Major Everett S. Simpson of Amarillo, Texas. Soldiers fell on the same soil that had soaked up American blood in World War I. In October 1918, not 90 miles away from this action on the Moselle, a battle blazed along the Aisne River. Twenty-six years earlier, Major Simpson's father, Captain Ethan Allen Simpson, was wounded and decorated with the Distinguished Service Cross. In a sober letter to his son, the elder Simpson wrote:

[I]f it is necessary for you to die in the faithful performance, the courageous performance of your duty, then you must not flinch. You must remember that this country of ours and its people and its institutions are worth dying for a thousand times.[14]

Riflemen, machine gunners, and ammunition carriers worked their way across, fighting the turbulent river swollen from freezing autumn rains. Inch by inch the 36th fought through Remiremont when resistance suddenly crumbled. The Germans were forced back, withdrew across the river, blowing the last remaining bridge. The T-Patchers had secured only one temporary bridge that spanned the Moselle, and seasonal rains had turned the river into a raging flood. Supporting units were just catching up to the swift advance of the 36th when a secure Moselle bridgehead appeared to stand firm. It was clear, however, that Nazi resistance had toughened and a continuous, slow-moving front unfolded.

The U.S. military was short of supplies in France, resulting in rationing of critical items like artillery ammunition and particularly gasoline to even combat units. The invaluable French Army felt abandoned and was embittered by the lack of logistical support. All units throughout France, however, suffered from shortages. The great battles from Normandy eastward and from Southern France to the northeast, had gobbled up a huge amount of supplies. On American soil, the emotional plea for conservation and the institution of ration coupons was no political move. Our boys overseas were in desperate need of fuel and munitions as the war drug them further north to endure another bitter winter.[15] Mindful of the long cold months advancing, Cecil turned to home for supplies to get them through.

Oct 5, 1944
Deep in France

Dear Dad & Veltie,

I am OK today, have a little cold but this letter is mostly business. I need a blast furnace like plumbers use. You know they burn gasoline like a blowtorch. Plumbers use them in melting lead and babbitt. I don't know how easy they will be to buy but maybe you can find one or buy it through someone. The next best thing would be a blow torch the bigger the better or two of them. If you found a torch and a furnace, that would be perfect. Second-hand might be alright. I will gladly pay for everything. Use this letter in mailing at post office. Grady Norris will understand that it is war equipment and it may weigh over 5 pounds. I have sent a picture to Veltie of our radio repair shop. I will appreciate it very much and explain all of the many uses later. Say hello to everyone.

Love,
Cecil

The above items are needed for the maintenance of battery electrical equipment.
—Theodore J. Stephany H.Q.F.A.

(The postscript was added by an officer of the Headquarters Field Artillery Unit to authorize the mailing of the blowtorch.)

After the Moselle River was crossed, a solid bridgehead was established, but there was to be no rest for the 36th Division. For seven long weeks the Texans struggled through the tedious, tiresome task of clearing German resistance out of the Vosges foothills between the Valogne and Meurthe Rivers to secure a line of departure for an attack over the Vosges passes. There were no great battles or excitement to ease the soldier's pain through the cold and tough terrain. The Germans fought bitterly to hold those hills, making progress painstakingly slow, often measured in yards. The fighting was not along roads and in towns but on rugged, heavily forested ridges, in flooded fields, and in mud. By October 12, the way was cleared in a line west of Docelles and much needed reinforcements began arriving. The 442nd Combat Team, comprised of Americans of Japanese descent, was attached to the 36th Division.[16]

Oct 12, 1944
France

Dearest Mom & Dad,

Once again, it's one of those occasions where I'm writing while there's a lull in the wee hours of the night. There's nothing of which to write about but I should let you know that I'm ok.

My last letter was from Coney. By now, I guess they are well settled on their new place. Herman will have a long way to go to work.

How do you think you will like the new road to Sweetwater?

Almost everyone seems to hear from Joyce pretty often. She writes me too. I sent her a little gift from France.

The war isn't over yet. That's all the news.

Hello to all.

Love,
Cecil

The war *was* a long way from finished, and the optimism expressed in letters just a few weeks earlier had given way to the sober realization that Allied Forces must pry German fingers off each stolen acre for the duration of the war. The 36th was spread widely over the Vosges Hills, but, with the addition of the Japanese-American unit, they had solid contact with friendly troops on both flanks of the Division for the first time since landing in France. A fresh attack began on October 15th. With splendid artillery support, the wide front line moved through the remnants of Bruyeres and wrestled the railroad track away from the Germans. A stinging defeat had been dealt to the Nazis.[17]

Oct. 15, 1944
Somewhere in France

Dearest Mom & Dad,

Your last letter came yesterday. You had been to see your girls the week before, Mom. Dad said the cotton would be pretty good if it would open.

Yes, I guess I am a long way from home and everybody.

The other nite I happened to be out in darkness so black you couldn't see your hand before you. The only light was the flash of the guns when they opened up. A night like that makes you think too much about that warm room back at home.

There's not a thing to write. I'm OK never felt better. I guess I'll be coming home someday if the trains still stop in Roscoe. Ha!

Hello Ava and H.C. Junior!

Goodnight,
Cecil

Oct. 16, 1944
Somewhere in France

Dearest Mom & Dad,

This Monday nite I'm ok again.

We had fried chicken for supper—Yum! Yum! This letter I'm writing so I can enclose this little newspaper. I have mentioned how our artillery made an 11 mile junk yard out of the war machine of the German 19th Army.

Someone must be seeding wheat at home about now. It's the middle of October.

Goodnite,
Cecil

    The little newspaper was not in Cecil's memoirs, so we can only guess the article was about the destruction of the fleeing Germans from the Battle of Montelimar. The route of the Nazi withdrawal was under fire for 16 miles. Long convoys were destroyed, and the entire zone was literally covered with a mass of burned vehicles, trains, equipment, dead animals and dead men.[18]

The Headquarters Battery often found housing often while in France. They were able to operate their radio communication indoors, which kept the equipment out of the rain and weather and gave Cecil a chance to make several French acquaintances. Some of these new friends were good to write him as the Texans continued their trek through Europe. Deacon Turner saved letters from grateful French friends who were concerned about his welfare and expressed their appreciation for how he and the Allies had given them back their country. In a letter postmarked "November 14th, 1944, Montelimar," a friend named "Odette" writes that her mother's wound is almost healed. "I and my family are well, aside from my youngest brother who has broken his leg playing football." French lives were certainly getting back to normal, with an American twist. In Cecil's journal, he mentioned the "Baur family" at Le Panges on two separate dates in October. He also stayed in Docelles and Bruyeres, meeting and enjoying the French locals.

Cecil (middle) and buddies with the children of a family that housed them at Docelles, France.

Uncle Cecil (left) letting children climb in an American jeep at Docelles, France.

Oct. 26, 1944
France

Dearest Mom & Dad,

Once more, I'm OK as can be. All is not so rough in France. Right now we have our radio station set up in a nice French family's home. They are as nice to us as nice can be. The lady told me she was 19 when the soldiers of World War I were in France and that she was proposed to a few times by American doughboys. They have a little boy 3 years old, a girl 15 and one 18. We feel so welcome here—sleep in beds, cook with them, however we eat about a quarter of a mile up the road at our battery kitchen. We call her "Mama" and the husband "Papa."

This is twelve hours later. I'm on the radio and it's 3:30 in the morning. The lady has asked us to all eat dinner with her tomorrow. She says we will have roast rabbit, fried potatoes, etc. Potatoes are grown here by the acre. The family brings the wood in for our fire and I keep it going half the time. Things are not so bad now but you never know what it will be like the next week.

The lady has made us a pie for dinner the last two days. The French are good cooks.

Say hello to everyone.

Love,
Cecil

Cecil beside a French farm home.

Cecil finds a pet in France.

Taking care of their camp pet with Robert Myer, San Antonio.

The wide front line had held in the seizure of Bruyeres and across the ridge to Biffontaine. The Corps commander decided, seeing German strength so badly shattered, it was time to make a big push to the north. The 36th Division held an impressive, ever-increasing section of the front, which led to their selection to extend an easterly spur into the German Corps mountain position. Execution of this mission resulted in one of the most dramatic episodes in the war—the "Lost Battalion" of the 141st Infantry.

Early morning on October 24, 1944, the 1st Battalion, 141st started its trek up the mountain. The hilltop ridge was heavily wooded, only a foot trail ran the seven kilometer length because of steep sides and deep gullies to the valley 1,000 feet below. Their advance went so well that German opposition was quickly overcome. By late afternoon, the head of the column had gone seven kilometers and reached its objective. A sudden enemy counterattack, striking from both sides, succeeded in severing the thin line stretched by the quick advance. Several Companies of the 1st Battalion were completely cut off from their Commander and the remaining unit. The 275 men had driven deep into enemy territory and were surrounded by Germans when the trail behind them was taken.[19]

Men of the 141st conducted themselves in the true tradition of their unit, which originated at The Alamo in Texas. The coded message that came into regimental headquarters that night said simply, "No rations, no water, no communications with headquarters . . . four litter cases."[20] The only bright spot which might see them through was that the Germans were unaware the Americans were there. In order to keep their secret, they had to limit fires and noise.[21]

Several attempts were made by trapped patrols to get out, and heroic troops from the 442nd (Nisei) Combat Team below tried to reach the hilltop, but the Germans had a heavy force. The "Lost Battalion" starved for five days, grubbing for mushrooms or trapping birds with little success. After several failed attempts at dropping supplies, the food-loaded shells and belly tanks with medical supplies and rations hit their mark. However, the planes and shells let the enemy in on the secret and on the sixth morning, the Germans attacked, expecting an easy kill. Armed with full bellies and the ammunition they had been saving for six days, the Americans made a miraculous stand that exacted a heavy toll on the overconfident Nazis. In the afternoon, a sergeant on outpost saw some movement in a bush below. He raised his rifle but waited until the helmeted figure came closer. He then dropped his rifle, ran down the slope, dancing, crying and hugging the surprised figure. At a loss for words, the American soldier of Japanese descent managed to ask, "Say, do you need any cigarettes?"[22] Unlike the war in the Pacific, the Japanese-American comrades were a welcomed sight indeed to the 211 survivors from the trapped battalion on this European front.

Oct 31, 1944 France
Dearest Mom & Dad–

Received your letter today written together and sent airmail Oct. 12. I have already received the Christmas box you packed for me.

We have eaten the chocolates and still have the pecan candy. The gloves are real nice and just what I hoped to receive before it gets too cold. I'll probably be putting on both pair of sox at once soon. Thank you very much for remembering the things I need.

No, Dad, I did not receive a medal with the citation, at first it was a Silver Star then ended in the citation you received. I am not interested in medals as much as I am in being Mr. Turner again.

I must go to bed now. I'll write again tomorrow and send some more money, maybe $100.

You will never know how much I enjoy the long letters you write.

Goodnight,
Cecil

P.S.—Nov. 3—Hello—I'm late with this letter!

The United Sates Postmaster General in 1944 ordered that overseas Christmas boxes be mailed early. Parents, wives and sweethearts quickly obeyed and yuletide came to the Vosges in mid-autumn. The Army mail clerk began his traditional December role in late October. The 36th Division Post Office handled many thousands of packages containing premature gifts of fruit cake, toilet articles, and woolen sweaters. Santa had been too fast that year.[23]

Cecil replied to his dad's inquiry about a medal that accompanied the citation. Everyday, Deacon Turner saw heroism and had just heard of the miraculous rescue of the courageous "Lost Battalion." Communication at Headquarters Battery was vital to the success of his division and he wanted to do everything to make their job swift and successful. Seeking medals and recognition was not even a fleeting thought to most soldiers as they went about their job of ridding the world of Nazis, then going home to their loved ones.

The Official After Action Reports for the 36th Division in November 1944 were quite lengthy as each numbered regiment was involved on a numbered hill in a numbered sector. The long paragraphs seem to contain more numerals than words. The cryptic, massive reports clearly reflect the type of war the doughboys faced that month. Lying before the weary T-Patchers was a sea of small and large hills, laced with mines, covered with dense foliage, with the enemy lurking behind every tree. Progress was slow as they edged their way down valleys and crawled up the next hill, continually forcing the enemy back until much of the forests were no longer standing. To cross the Vosges from west to east, against a determined enemy, had been tried in several ancient and more recent exploits—but none successful. The 36th Division was the first combat unit in history to accomplish this feat. Much of the success of the T-Patchers was due to the heroic efforts of the combat engineers who managed to build a miraculous road through the hills. A lifeline of supplies and medical relief flowed through these passages.

At the back door of the house Cecil helped build to protect the radio equipment during the winter of 1944 in France.

Nov. 4, 1944
France

Dearest Mom & Dad,

Tonite finds me doing fine and wondering how everything goes at home.

I have been building, actually doing a little carpenter work the last three days. One man and myself have built a little house on a small truck to put the radio station in this winter. We have it all finished except the top which we will cover with real heavy tarp or canvas. It has three glass windows in it and a door in the back. I will try to send pictures of it. It sure will be a help when it gets down below zero this winter. I will fire up the furnace that you and Veltie are sending me. It should be easy to heat since it's so small.

I can't tell you and Veltie how much I do appreciate your sending me the furnace. Tell Veltie he must write all about how much trouble it was to find one, the price, etc. etc. Where did you buy it? Only winter will tell just how much it really will be worth to me. It should be here before long.

Yes, Dad, I get the Roscoe Times pretty good but it skips now and then and is pretty old sometimes. The last one I got had the story of Joe Windham and his 50 missions over Europe.

I am enclosing $100 more, Dad, so you let me know if you get it.

I hate to hear that you and Mom are listening for the

siren. I am optimistic myself but please don't try to hold your breath until the war ends.

Mom, I suppose there have been a few things happening to make you blue or disappointed judging from your last letter. I don't know the situation or the circumstances as I have been away from home, actually four years but as far as I am personally concerned, I have still in my memory the letter you wrote to me when you first married Dad. Something like, "I have a personal interest in every one of you children and want to try to be a mother to you. I want to try to win all of you." Now then, Mom, as long as you have a good motive and someone else's interest at heart in every little thing you do or say then you need not worry about the outcome. As for me, I will consider you a good mother until you prove otherwise.

That's all for tonite.

Love always,
Cecil

A farm boy brings to the Army all kind of skills that perhaps many of the big city soldiers never had a chance to learn. On a farm, building stock pens and housing with scrap lumber was a normal task. It was probably fun and even therapeutic for Cecil to build the little enclosure for the radio equipment. With houses no longer available, vital communication gear was exposed to the increasingly cold elements in these French hills.

Many Americans today are unaware that our homeland was definitely under threat from the enemy during the war. The enemy planned to invade from the Pacific and Atlantic. Many communities held siren drills to prepare for the possibility of invasion. It was difficult enough for Sergeant Turner to see the lovely French villages destroyed by the Nazis, but even more upsetting to think of the same destruction at home. Cecil encouraged his family not to be fearful. Even though the end of the war was not yet in sight, he was confident the Allies had a righteous cause and would prevail.

Cecil was blessed with a faithful stepmother, so diligent to write as months turned into years. There must have been some problem with acceptance by the other children, however, from the consolation he was offering his "Mom." His letters frequently requested the status of everything at home, but it seems almost petty to lay this strife on him while in a daily life and death struggle. Still, Cecil used insightful, sweet words of encouragement and the problem was evidently not mentioned again.

Nov 6, 1944
Somewhere in France

Dad and Mom,

If you think I can write you in five minutes then you are right. I'm doing fine and getting ready to go to bed for five hours sleep. I got your letter of Oct. 8. Yes, Dad, I will keep an eye on all the Krauts in haylofts and every place else. I will give you an example: One of our boys was out on a telephone line when he captured a German and he made the prisoner help him fix the line.

Thank you, for the box you have mailed. I'm glad you sent the gloves and sox. I started to request them but it's no longer necessary as they are on the way.

I'll write again later maybe in the morning.

I'm sleepy.

Goodnight,
Cecil

The Campaign in the Vosges resembled the muddy fighting in Italy. Rain gave way to snow, multiplying hardships on the soldier. Life on the front line was miserable.[24] A new replacement brought to the front in early November described what he saw, "The men were a rough looking crew. They all had long, shaggy hair, a few days' growth of whiskers, dirty combat clothes . . ."[25]

Throughout October and early November of 1944, the battle was painfully slow with limited rewards. However, against the bitter odds of weather and terrain, the elusive enemy finally began to retreat, piling up obstacles and leaving a path of charred destruction.[26]. Cecil mentions, "Germans burned all the town at Corcieux" in his journal. Another T-Patcher remembers, " . . . we saw our first 'scorched earth' towns. St. Die flared brightly at night."[27]

Nov 7, 1944
France

Dearest Mom & Dad,

Here's a short note for tonite to let you know I'm doing OK in every way.

I had a package from Aunt May. She is really nice to me.

I saw Pete Buckner and talked to him a few weeks ago. He was doing fine.

Politics are pretty active over here alright, Dad, and the fellows take a pretty good interest.

There's nothing new this time.

All my love,
Cecil

Hello Ava & Clay baby!

More than two weeks passed before Cecil found time to send another letter home. His short journal entry for November 26, 1944 summarized the efforts of the Texans during these weeks—"Surprised Germans at St. Marie." The U. S. Army, poised all along the Vosges, prepared to descend into the Alsace plains if a way could be found through the high mountain passes. Many of the narrow gaps were targeted with concentrated German defenses. Marie Pass was a formidable obstacle at an altitude of over 2,900 feet. Only one tiny road zigzagged along the cleft of the mountain that led up to the high village. The enemy had positioned heavy timber road blocks at the high point in the road, elaborate trenches and wire systems on the hillsides flanking the road, and deep dugouts for the garrison. From the top of the Pass, the enemy commanded full observation of the road below.[28]

The haze of a frosty late autumn morning hung over St. Marie Pass on November 25th. Under cover of the misty atmosphere, a small force moved up the road to the pass. At the same time, the remainder of a battalion circled around several miles to the left over terrain so rugged that no artillery, no armor, and no vehicles could accompany them. After four hours of climbing, armed only with what they could carry, they approached St. Marie from the rear.

Racing down from the hills, their arrival was a complete surprise. German soldiers were captured riding bicycles on the streets and the only struggle occurred at the railroad station. By late afternoon, St. Marie was entirely taken by the 36th. One hundred seventy prisoners were taken in the town while our troops suffered only two minor injuries.

Artillery fire took out the German garrison below the pass so the engineers could begin to clear the roadblocks. Before nightfall, several units triumphantly marched down the road through the pass. Throughout centuries of history, no army had been able to penetrate this narrow gap. On November 24, 1944 the impossible happened.

> The highest, narrowest, and toughest pass of the Vosges had thus been breached. This was the one the Germans thought impregnable. In a whining bleat, the German communiqué reported that overwhelming forces had driven back their defenses at St. Marie. Actually, they had not been driven back but destroyed, and by a single battalion numbering less than 500 effectives which had consummated one of the riskiest and most brilliant maneuvers of the war. St. Marie had fallen, the crest of the Vosges had been passed, the gateway to the Alsace Plain swung open.[29]

The heading of Deacon Turner's next letter expresses new optimism spreading among the 36th following their victory at St. Marie — "France, almost liberated." Cecil also mentions moving closer to Berlin as the Allies hoped soon to be taking the fight to Hitler's front door. Much was happening in the Division but Turner's letters still focused on home —- what was happening in the Presidential election and his family there. The citation mentioned was awarded to his battery for their role in the invasion of Italy, liberation of Rome, and continued pursuit of the enemy.

Nov. 24, 1944
France almost liberated

Dearest Mom & Dad,

I have received your V-mail letter of Nov. 8 and glad you have gotten the wooden shoes. They are by no means valuable except as a souvenir of France. I had never seen a wooden shoe until I came to France.

I can't have the mom write to you because we have moved on closer to Berlin. If I go back that way by any chance I will have her write to you.

No, I did not vote. It's not the right attitude but I told the fellows I knew Roosevelt would win. I did know it. Regardless of what some people said and predicted I knew he would win.

The reason the checks are still $40 is I decided to send the extra money home by money order. By now you have gotten the $100 check I sent about the 4th or 5ᵗʰ of Nov.

I am sending this citation to you for our battery of about 96 men given by the division commander.

I'm expecting the torch any day now. I got a real nice box from Bobbie Wash.

Hello there Ava & H.C. Is Joyce still with you. I wonder

*if she got the little gift I sent her. I have sent everyone
something from overseas.*

That's all for now.

Love,
Cecil

HEADQUARTERS 36TH INFANTRY DIVISION
APO #36, U.S. Army
7 October 1944

SUBJECT: Divisional Citation of Unit
TO: Commanding Officer, Headquarters and
Headquarters Battery, 36th Infantry Division Artillery,
APO #36, U.S. Army

The Headquarters and Headquarters Battery, 36th
Infantry Division Artillery, is cited for exceptional performance in action from 25 May to 26 June 1944 in Italy.

CITATION

Headquarters and Headquarters Battery, 36th Infantry Division Artillery, for exceptional performance from 26
May to 26 June 1944 in the monumental 29-day push from
the Anzio beachhead area through Rome to the hills over-
looking Pisa. During the attack on the stubbornly defended
stronghold of Velletri, Headquarters and Headquarters
Battery, 36th Infantry Division Artillery coordinated the
fires of the artillery battalions, successfully completing
the delicate mission of blasting enemy positions in Velletri
without endangering friendly troops above and below the
city. After Velletri fell, the Division Artillery pressed on to
Rome and participated in the triumphal march through the

Eternal City. When the demoralized enemy forces crossed the Tiber, the Division continued forward in swift pursuit. In spite of the difficulties of communications and traffic control imposed by the speed of the advance, Division Artillery maintained close contact with the infantry regiments and, with from eight to six artillery battalions under its direct control, was constantly prepared to render effective support to the infantry troops.

John E. Dahlquist
Major General, U.S. Army
Commanding

St. Marie Pass and the Vosges had been breached for the first time in military history. Lieutenant General Alexander M. Patch, Seventh Army Commander, commending the 36th Division wrote:

In the Vosges foothills, you dislodged a desperate and skillful foe from positions which gave him every natural advantage. You fought for weeks to pave the way for a breakthrough. Despite unfavorable weather, terrain and savage resistance, you pushed on with tenacious courage.[30]

Tired by its long, arduous campaign, the 36th still had enough punch to burst onto the Alsace Plain and capture the important towns of Ribeauville and Selestat. Cecil recorded in his journal, "Big Stuff" at Ribeauville where "Braidwood and Mitchell" were killed. The first two weeks of December brought many casualties as the Nazis countered with a final push to keep the Allies out of Germany.

Dec 1, 1944
France

Dearest Mom & Dad,

Once again, I'm OK and it's after three in the morning. Things are quiet. It can't be noisy all the time. Everything is about the same with me. I think I have waited a little longer this time to write but maybe you'll forgive me.

Are you keeping a cow where you are now?

Ava will chew my ear I haven't written her lately. Well I hope to be there before too long to help mow the lawn etc.

I must go start the gasoline motor and go to bed.

Always remember me in your prayers.

Love,
Cecil

T-Patchers occupied the snow covered plain while the zigzag front line was anything but secure. Pockets of resistance were flaring up in surrounding hill villages. Fatigue to exhaustion crept in as no reserves were sent to relieve the Texans.

Dec 4, 1944
France

Dearest Mom & Dad,

This Dec. 4 finds me doing fine and hoping you are the same. Had a package today from Coney and she included some paper shelled pecans off of her new farm–ranch.

(Later)I found this letter that I had never finished so here's a few more lines on Dec. 15. I'm alright and hope all of you are the same and I hope you have a very happy Xmas. I think the tree for everybody is nice and a good idea.

Dad, the torch works like a house on fire–really good. You can take the $10 out of one of my checks.

In your last letter, Dad was trying to buy the Parker home–an airmail letter.

Maybe I'm late but–Merry Xmas!

All my love,
Cecil

Cecil (left) with young French friend and Bill Hutchins by the "house" built on the back of army truck to protect radio equipment. (note the vent to accommodate the torch-furnace)

With the arrival of Cecil's $10 torch, the radio work was literally housed in the heated bed of the truck, out of the damaging winter elements. The ingenious resourcefulness of Cecil and the radio crew provided vital and undisturbed communication for the Division through the long winter months. His colloquial description of the torch's effectiveness, "like a house on fire," is a humorous although perhaps unintentional pun. It must have been an interesting scene to observe Newt Turner taking the large box in to mail his soldier in Europe and writing "blowtorch" on the contents label. The Roscoe postmaster had something indeed to tell his wife that evening around the supper table.

The 36th would spend the holiday season in snow-covered forests rivaling the most picturesque of Christmas cards, but Cecil could only dream of the treeless, flat plains of Texas. His fourth Christmas away from home was as hard, if not harder, than the first.

An unexpected change in momentum on the front caused the delay in finishing Cecil's letter. The Germans switched suddenly from the defensive to strike with all their might at both flanks of the Division line. Two days before the letter was sent, on that bloody December 13, the T-Patchers were surrounded. All along the foothills, the 36th was in danger of being completely overrun.

The entire student body of a German officer candidate school, at least 100 strong, attempted to envelope the Division flank and reach the Ribeauville-St. Marie Road. Had they succeeded in this, the 36th Division would have possibly been destroyed. Platoons and companies were temporarily surrounded. Men used bayonets and hand grenades to kill Germans at the edge of their foxholes. Everyone was committed, even headquarters personnel.[31]

Battalion after battalion counterattacked and forced the Nazis back. By middle of the afternoon of Dec. 13th, German raids had been repulsed all along the front. Hitler's forces had paid dearly with their lives and the next day's attempts were much less vigorous. In just two days, the German effort was ended and the almost 7,000 Nazi infantry brought across the Rhine for this effort had been killed, wounded, arrested, or chased back across the Rhine.

The 36th Division also paid a high price during the struggle. No single day of the fall and winter battles was recorded without lengthy casualty lists. In the combined battles of the Vosges and southern Alsatian campaigns, there were more than 6,000 casualties.[32]

Dec 15, 1944 France
My dear Sis, (I'll think of you & all when you have the tree.)

How is little Clay Jr. today. Tell him his Uncle Cec is doing OK. I have been too busy to write anyone very much. I had a letter started to Veltie for 6 days before I finished it.

Ava, now I know why your package was so long getting here. The censor probably had to spend several days checking on the contents. They probably thought it was a time bomb. Seriously tho' I never did see so much "stuff" in a box. You sure know how to pack a box and the right stuff to put in one. I feel like a civilian again. What with, Jergens lotion, hair oil, powder, blades, cream, etc. etc. I am a civilian! Let this letter be dedicated to telling you I'm ok and that the box you sent was a very nice gift and I appreciate it to no end.

Remember me in your prayers. Love,
Cecil

P.S. The divinity was divine!

Deacon Turner wrote his faithful sister the same day as his parent's last letter. The harrowing experiences of the past few days renewed his request for prayer once more. The 36th had foiled an attempt to separate the First French Army from the Seventh Army and annihilate the 36th Division.

On December 21, the Texans assumed command of the less active sector of Strasbourg. Battalion by battalion was relieved from the front line. For the first time since landing in France on August 15, Cecil and the 36th could briefly rest after 133 lengthy days of combat.

Dec 21, 1944
Europe

Dearest Mom & Dad,

I'm writing you another one of those letters while I'm operating radio, only this time I'm not sleeping. Several newspapers came today both SW and Roscoe papers and I had a letter from Aunt May. She is very good to write me and I received a Xmas package from her. Ava's package came and it was chucked full of everything–really nice.

This letter won't be there in time but I'm wishing all of you a Merry Christmas and a joyous New Year. Say hello to everybody and I hope you enjoyed the tree you had planned.

I'm always tickled pink to get a letter telling in detail

what you have been doing. Both of you apologize for your writing but it's easy to read.

All my love,
Cecil

The towering Cathedral still standing in the middle of bombed-out Strasbourg, France.

The best holiday present any of the Texans received in December of 1944 was relief from the front line and a hot bath. Strasbourg was a far more pleasant spot to spend Christmas than San Pietro had been the year before. T-Patchers were given five precious days there with the simple duty of paroling the quiet, medieval streets in search of German stragglers and agents. The Christmas church service was held in the majestic cathedral, miraculously spared from the bombing destruction so much of Strasbourg had suffered. On December 25, the soldiers organized a party for the children of Strasbourg. It must have seemed more like Christmas as they handed out treats from the baskets of hard candy and over 400 chocolate bars donated from the GI's packages from home. It was the first candy most of the children had tasted in over four years and in gratitude, they sang "Silent Night" and "O Holy Night." Angelic choirs could not have surpassed the soul-soothing medicine of children's voices in the Texans' ears so weary of gunfire.

Christmas Postcard

Dec 26, 1944

My Dear Dad & Mom,

I received your airmail letter written on Dec. 5. I hope you and everyone got all of your cotton before too much bad weather.

Dad, you seem a little worried about the Krauts using gas. Don't worry cause we are all equipped. Right now as I write this letter I can reach out and touch a gas mask. I believe they are too smart to use gas. No, I have not seen anything of their "Ray-bombs."

I think I can write more now and the next few days, but

now I will go to bed. Your letter was nice Mom. I had a real nice Christmas dinner.

Love,
Cecil

Cecil was in the city that founded the Christmas tree tradition while his family was gathered around theirs in Roscoe. Cotton farmers could be harvesting their crop from Thanksgiving to Christmas, depending on when the freeze killed the plants and the cotton bolls finished opening and could be stripped. If bad weather set in, delays could cause holiday meals and gatherings to be scheduled around work in the fields and trips to the gin.

Newt must have read and heard rumors of new bombs and gas the Germans were preparing in desperation. Cecil tried to reassure them that he and all the Americans were well prepared for all the "Krauts" might throw at them. But the home front was not the only one facing fears fed by rumors. The 36th was soon to enter a war phase where the enemy used propaganda and clandestine methods not seen before.

The initial plan was to let the 36th pull even further back from the line for a true rest near Sarrebourg. Rest for the entire Division never materialized. An urgent summons arrived: Germans were attacking just to the north. Three regiments quickly prepared an alternating strategy. While one directly engaged the enemy, another dug field emplacements along a switch line in case the Krauts penetrated too deeply. The third was in reserve, prepared to repulse German columns which had driven across the Rhine and established a sizeable bridgehead just north of Strasbourg. In addition, the entire 36th Division, the only reserve force in the Seventh Army, was prepared for immediate action in any sector. The installation of the switch line, a secondary defense point to stop the German advance in case they broke through the line, emphasized the seriousness of the situation. The next few weeks would determine the length and outcome of the war. While much of the Allied Army was embroiled in the struggle on the northeastern front in the "Battle of the Bulge," the Germans were also searching for a "bulge" in their southern front. The Americans inched too close to the German border and the Nazis were coiling to strike back with new venom.[33]

There was so much Cecil had experienced and perhaps needed to be able to share with someone close to him. It might have helped him deal with all he had been through but he knew it would not have helped his loved ones. All those discussions would have to wait until the guns were silenced and America's sons were allowed to go home.

Cecil in France, Winter 1944

Dec. 29, 1944
Europe

My Dear Mom & Dad,

Your letter written on the back of the Xmas Card came today and I enjoyed it very much.

Yes Dad, we all thought there would be very few soldiers in Europe when we wrote last Xmas. The war has lasted longer than we thought I guess.

Mom, you can look on the calendar and find Dec. 29 and say that Cecil was doing fine that evening and was quite comfortable. All is not misery overseas but all nites are not like tonite.

When we have a chance we will discuss everything after the War. You should see the number of books I got from Burton-Lingo (Sweetwater)—suggestions for new homes. Say if a fellow comes by to see you named Kinlock Kole from Breckenridge treat him swell. I don't have much suggestion on what you could do but just treat him as nice as possible. He was my radio sergeant before he went home for his health.

All my love,
Cecil

In his journal Cecil mentions a "Chateau burned" at Niederville in early January and "88's cold" at Montbronn, the center of communication for the 36th. The intense cold for the next few weeks required a three-day rotation of duty on the front line. However, the blowtorch had made a mobile radio post possible during the worst weather. Cecil found other uses for the torch as well.

Jan. 8, 1945

Somewhere in France

My Dear Dad, Mom & all,

I will write most of this to you, Dad, as I have been thinking of you so much lately and I may not get to write everyone so I will just say "Dear Everyone." The last time I wrote I spoke of having more time and taking it kinda easy then. It's quite a different story now and I'm quite busy.

The ole big torch is coming in handy in many ways. You should have seen us the other day. We ran onto some potatoes in our dug out and cooked part of them. A French woman gave us about a half gallon of milk (I gave her some cigarettes for her husband) so we had quite a feast including some fruitcake that Mae Wheeler sent me.

I'm getting kinda used to the cold weather. France is not as cold as I thought it would be. We have a lot of warm clothing. You should see some of my sox. I think some of them must weigh a pound each.

I noticed where Pete Buckner captured a bunch of Jerries and had his name in the paper again.

Do you plan to farm any next year since you have gotten rid of your tractor this year I mean?

I got a letter from my French girl today. She lives way back in Southern France and her brother wrote it in English and I read it easy enough. I hope to see her again.

That's all for now.

All my love,
Cecil

P.S. Mom, will you apologize to everyone for me. I just haven't written anyone.

Goodnight,
Cecil

Cecil finds a rest stop in war-torn France, 1945.

According to the Official After Action Reports, the communications headquarters for the 36th Division was housed at Montbronn during early January. Cecil must not have stayed there during this period, however, because his journal mentions "Hagenau—nuns want to go with us." Hagenau was a site for an intense struggle between the Texans and "Jerry" over many days. Even Strasbourg was at risk as the enemy pushed to regain control of this notch of France that extended down to Colmar and bordered Germany to the north and east. With a foot of snow falling at times, the 36th had to whitewash tanks and reverse the white lining out of parkas while some wore ghostly draped bed sheets.

After a year and a half of fighting the Germans, some Texans noticed a change in the expected fighting behavior of the Nazis. One T-Patcher described them as "mad drunk" as the fighting took on an enemy fanaticism new to the war. An explanation developed as treacherous SS troops were captured, forcing new levels of caution against the devious sect. Nazis were using American tanks as well as dressing in American and British uniforms. For many, the first few weeks and months of 1945 were the worst of the war. Their job was to strengthen a thinly spread defense line that was continually being hacked away.[34]

One T-Patcher quickly recalled this juncture:

"It was like trying to straighten out five miles of twisted rail after a train wreck. Along our line there were gaps to be filled, isolated squads or platoons to save, tanks to be met, and terrorizing reports to be checked out and dismissed as fables, or met with hurried strength if found to be true. It was evident that 'Jerry' had his mind made up to go someplace, and though we might change his mind at noon, there was nothing to assure us that nightfall wouldn't find him with the same idea."[35]

The wire patrol still had a vital and dangerous job to keep communication flowing for the thinly spread troops. France 1945

January 24, 1945
Somewhere in some part of France

Dearest Mom & Dad,

I hope you will understand and will forgive me for being so long in writing but I know you understand. I remember I promised to write every day once. I found that was impossible but I do write every chance I get. I know you wouldn't want me to neglect my duty to write.

Your letters are always an inspiration and I'm always watching the mail for one.

I wish I could tell you all about what I'm doing and what I have seen and where I have been but if there were no regulations I wouldn't be able to. I'm out of the habit of writing and I find it hard to describe anything.

I'm still working with radio and artillery.

I'm doing ok so be good and write often and I will try to do the same.

Love,
Cecil

More than two weeks had passed since the Turners had heard from their son. Cecil apologized but acknowledged that his naïve pledge to write every day was made before the enemy made it impossible. As if the new impetus of the enemy wasn't enough, another T-Patcher writes,

> We were now fighting in a section of France where many of its people were sympathetic with the Nazis. In one instance, a whole-scale plot to sabotage our defensive positions and routes of communication was uncovered. Curfews were set and strictly enforced. We could trust no one. The most haggard refugee might well be an enemy agent slipping through to scout our positions.[36]

With several different outfits in the same sector, including some French, signs and countersigns became an important part of the operation. Another crucial combat innovation, introduced by the 36th, was the anti-aircraft searchlight. At times pointed toward the line several thousand yards away, it proved extremely productive in watching for movement of the enemy.

At the end of January, the Russian's sweeping gains on the Eastern Front forced the Germans to halt further operations on the Alsace plain. Enemy initiative died out noticeably just before the Division spotted movement of enemy troops away from the northeast corner of France. The Texans, with no time to celebrate the victory, prepared for another full-scale attack on the retreating Germans[37]

Letter writing was put on hold as the 36th was engaging the enemy with a new tenacity. Cecil has many entries in his journal during late January and into the next few months of this phase where there was no pause from the heavy fighting. He writes, "100,000,000,000 mm 'Alsace Alice'–Brumoth" and mentions other towns, "Winterhausen, Pfaffenhoffen, Soultz, Wissembourg, and Bergzabern." The day before he wrote the following letter, he writes, "Boom! Radio Planes! Are we alone?"

February 1, 1945
Somewhere in France

My Dear Mom & Dad,

I must take this opportunity to let you know that I am OK while my hands are clean and I have a little time on my hands. I have no complaints to make except a complaint to file against the Germans who have upset the entire world. Maybe we will have them upset before too long.

It's after supper now and I will finish this letter. The mail just came in and I had a letter from Ava, Joyce, Veltie, Mozelle, and two newspapers. It was nice to hear that everyone was OK again. I was certainly sorry to hear about Aubrey Stewart.

Dad, I am enclosing another $100 you can deposit for me. That should buy some seed wheat–Ha! Let me know when you get it.

I enjoyed the two pictures Joyce sent me of her, Ava, and Clay. I always enjoy pictures. If you have any made of any kind–send me some. I would emphasize that too if I thought it would help.

I had a letter from Coney too. She received the little gift I had sent her. I have sent everyone something while I have been overseas.

I'm sure the news is sure making everyone feel a lot better these days.

This is all for tonite.

Love,
Cecil

Cecil's complaint against the Nazis would intensify as the war continued and more of their dark character was brought to light. Although he could not write about the battles he had lived through, he hoped their victories were encouraging his loved ones.

Feb 4, 1945
France

Dearest Mom & Dad,

Your letter of Jan. 16 rolled in today–the one that Ava helped write. My spirits are up tonite. I got 3 letters.

This is another one of those letters to let you know I'm alright. Just writing before I go to bed. It's nearly 12 o'clock and I came off duty at 12 (midnight)

We are in a house this time. I'm operating the radio. I have just started the little motor to charge the battery. I have just gotten the all clear from the site and broadcast it out to all the others. It was only one enemy plane and wasn't too close.

That's all I know tonite. The news is good and I know that means a lot to you.

Be good and have some chicken when I get home.

Love,
Cecil

For the first half of February, the 36th Division was involved in battles all along the Moder River. Suffering heavy casualties and a crumbling situation on the Eastern front, the German's offensive position faded away. Only in pockets were they able to maintain some stubborn defensive action. In the town of Oberhoffen, the Germans gave a little, counterattacked often, and held out for nearly two weeks. An early thaw complicated movement as the Moder River bordering the city flooded beyond its banks. Water flowed over the engineers' bridges, and fields of snow turned into swamps all the way to the Rhine. Movement to and from the city was slowed to wading speed. In town, fierce house to house and even room to room battles took place.[38] One veteran of the action said, "For a month, we moved east and west, but never very far north."[39]

Feb 12, 1945
France

My Dear Dad & Mom,

Just a few words to let you know I'm ok on this nite of Feb 12.

I'm on duty at the radio now and I come off at 12 o'clock and that's only five minutes from now so I'll just say hello and goodbye.

Say hello to all for me. Both of you don't work too hard!

Love,
Cecil

Feb. 20, 1945
Somewhere in France

My Dear Mom & Dad,

All the other fellows are gone and all the little Piper Cub planes are back on the ground now. They didn't see very much today while they were flying around up there so we didn't have very much to shoot at.

I believe in your last letter the two of you had about finished with the trees and shrubs and Auti & Agnes had been over for a waffle supper.

Nothing extraordinary has been happening to me—everything about the same.

You seem to like your new home. Why don't you draw me a floor plan of how its built on a sheet of paper and enclose it in one of your letters? Did I ever tell you that we fellows like to plan and discuss homes when we get a little time off? I received a large bundle of books on planning a home. All of them have floor plans, pictures of the home after completion etc. etc.

We had a nice meal tonight–beefsteak being the main attraction so you see we are getting plenty to eat.

I had a letter from a good friend in Southern France with whom I stayed during the "Battle of Montelimar." He is a cousin of the school teacher I write to back there. He was recalling memories of the fight that went on around his home and expressing his thanks for the Americans liberating Southern France. I will write to him soon and maybe to his cousin again–you can't tell!

It's about time I should wake up someone to take my place, so–

Goodnight. Love,
Cecil

Feb. 25, 1945
Somewhere in Alsace

Dear Dad & Mom,

This evening finds me doing OK and feeling alright.

I had one letter today and was really glad to get it–it was from Veltie.

He said that Joyce was married to Norris. Do you know more about it? He knew no more than that. Does Joyce still have the job at the bank? It sounded like a good job.

I'll probably get a letter from you soon as it has been some time since the last one. Veltie said everyone was alright. That's good.

We are still pounding the "Boche."

I wish I could tell you when I would be home then I would know myself—ha!

All my love,
Hello Ava and Clay! Cecil

They were "pounding the 'Boche'" but not without a cost. The men were weary, wet and cold. Most of the 36th were shuffled in and out of Bains-les-Bains during the end of February for a short rest.

Cecil was surprised to hear his baby sister, Joyce, had gotten married. She had written fairly often so this marriage must have been pretty sudden. He didn't want to perhaps make matters worse by reacting negatively in the letter home. The topic is just slipped in and then he hurried on to responding to a question about coming home. Cecil's family continued to change in his absence: loss of his mother and grandmother, babies born, houses burned, and now he alone was unmarried among all of Newt Turner's children.

March 1, 1945
Somewhere in Alsace

My dear Mom & Dad,

The box of Pangburn's Chocolates arrived in very good shape today and they are very good. Pardon me while I pause to eat one. I appreciate it very much. I believe that was Ava's handwriting on the package meaning that she had a hand in it too. That's three people I am grateful to for making life a little more pleasant for me. I don't want you to ever go through any great inconvenience to send me anything. Remember I will always get by without these nice things but they do mean a lot to us. We get nearly everything we need. In my pocket right now I have the tiny little tube of lip-ice for my lips that do chap pretty often. Ava sent it Christmas. If you ever need a request, use this letter.

I am mailing a package home in the morning. It has a large ashtray made of glass and some picture postcards from away back. If you like the ashtray, use it around your home. Some day I might like to have it to go in my home, if I ever have one, since it has "Made in Berlin" on it. Give the cards to Veltie. He is keeping a lot of overseas "stuff" for me.

I had a letter from Joyce and when I noticed the name of the addressee, Mrs. O.C. Norris. I wondered why Mrs. Norris was writing to me. Now I remember that Clark was named after his grandfather. Joyce said she was very happy. I hope so. It is a confused World to be getting married in but I guess it's ok as far as I know. I have heard of him a lot but I'm not sure that I've ever seen him. Anyway, I have too much more to occupy my mind over here so I'll have to let the people fight the war at home while I look after myself over here. I'm the baby now! The only child left!

Your European son,
Always pray for me—Love—Cecil

His sister's marriage must have been a hot family topic but Cecil needed to focus on the job at hand—finishing off the Nazis with a push across the border. Most of the large German force in the south had been pulled back across the border but some pockets of resistance still had to be cleared in many of the Alsace villages.

March 3, 1945
Somewhere in Alsace

My dear Mom & Dad,

Maybe by this time you have completely recovered from your ailment and I was very sorry to hear of it. I have been sick just about enough in my life to make me always feel for others when they are ill. Take care of yourself, Mom, that's an order. Cause I'm a sergeant. Ha!

Things have been very much the same with me for a long time now. I simply cannot complain.

I had a letter from Irene and one from Betty Jo. She is in school at Denton. Betty sent me a number of pictures and I really enjoyed them. There was one of Aubrey. You know I have not seen him in years. I don't know how many. Clara finished high school this year.

I'm glad to hear that you aren't working too hard maybe, Dad, since you are only going to have 100 acres of wheat.

It would make me mad if I knew you two worried about me any. If it comes time to worry, I will let you know. Ha!

Don't forget about tending to the chicks tonite.

All my Love,
Cecil

Talk of home and feeding chicks helped Sgt. Turner escape from the stress, even if just for a few minutes. He tried to reassure his folks with his light-hearted banter. Cecil was burdened with the knowledge that his precarious, life-threatening position resulted in a hardship on his anxious family. The age and health of his father produced an even greater motivation to shield him from additional stress caused by his youngest son's military service. It also motivated Cecil to keep his promise of frequent letters, in spite of conditions of which his family would never totally become aware.

Town by town the 36th continued to secure the Alsace plain. The Germans continued to fight in this area, even when it appeared they would be cut off from the heartland by the driving force of Patton's Third Army. It was a determined, desperate fighting force that opposed the Texans in the battles of March 1945.[40]

March 10, 1945
Somewhere in Alsace

My Dear Mom & Dad,

This night finds me feeling fine. I have just been waked up to work my shift on the radio. We have one less tonite on duty because he went to rest camp. You remember I wrote to you about going to rest camp in Rome and Paserta while I was in Italy. This one is about like them only I hear it's better. It's about 7 days of complete rest where it's quiet and peaceful. I have not been yet but I may some day. I don't need a rest as bad as some of the boys.

Two letters came yesterday from you, writing on the 24th and 26th of Feb. I'm glad you were some better, mom, and sitting up. I waited for your letters, Dad.

If you don't hear from me for seven days that does not

mean anything. I'll try to write more often and make a trade with you—I'll notify you when its time to worry ok? Ha!

Say hello to all for me. Remember me.

Love,
Cecil

Bains-le-Bains had been turned into a rest camp for a few months. After shedding their mud-stained combat clothes, a hot shower, and donning a complete new uniform, the men were fed a chef-prepared dinner. The next luxury was to crawl between white sheets, the first for many soldiers in over a year. Cecil never mentioned Bains-les-Bains in his journal or his letters. Perhaps there were not enough replacements for all the radio operators to get a break.

Before the end of March, Alsace had been cleared of the Nazi invaders and rear troops were now taking up the job of policing the area while the 36th moved on for their final conquest.

March 11, 1945
In Alsace

Dearest Dad & Mom,

This Sunday nite finds me on duty and I'm feeling great. The food is good enough and I'm healthy. I am pleased with the way my teeth are responding to my attention. I had neglected them for a while and now I am whipping them—back in shape. Yes, Dad, the war will be over some day sudden like and we will wonder why we thought the end was so far away.

I am sorry if you didn't get news from me for seven days. Something more important took the mail, I guess. Don't worry about me. I'm OK. I'm glad to hear the wheat is looking good. I guess I'm a wheat grower at heart.

May the Lord Bless and protect you in everything you do everyday. Remember me.

Love,
Cecil

Dental hygiene was important to Cecil his entire life. He could wear out a toothbrush in just a few days. It is amusing, however, that he would talk about the condition of his teeth while all Allied Forces were coordinating efforts for the push into Germany for the final death blow.

A common fear among soldiers was their loved ones at home would have days go by without even a thought of them. He ended on a solemn note with a prayer blessing on his family and the familiar admonition to those he loved so well to "remember me" in their prayers and thoughts.

The discussion Deacon Turner had with his father on how the war would suddenly be over was to be prophetic. Little did both Cecil and his dad know how soon the simple exchange of rhetoric would be realized.

Cecil wrote the next letter while still in France. By then, the first boots of the 36th were already covered with German soil. The water border was crossed on the 19th of March and the Texans were preparing to punch through the famous Siegfried line. The 36th Headquarters with Cecil's unit would follow soon after.

March 22, 1945
Alsace

Dear Mom & Dad,

This March 22 finds me OK and I have been getting your letters regularly now. I have the drawing of the layout of your home already and a number of V-mails. I think the two things I liked most were the weeping willow tree over so much evergreen hedge. No wonder you like your home. — The outside entrance to the front bedroom.

I had a letter today from Georgia and two from Hubert the other day. It's nice to get mail again regularly. I was glad to hear that you are almost well again, Mom, and don't go to getting sick again. Ha!

Don't forget to send me some of the next pictures you have made if any.

Say hello to Bro. Elrod for me, Dad.

Love,
Cecil

It must have been difficult to restrain sharing with his family the fear and excitement the troops felt as they moved into what had to be the final phase of the war. Instead, he kept his mind occupied and letters busy with talk of house plans.

The 36th Division had played a large role in the liberation of France. The only obstacle remaining was to engage the enemy on his home field with no underground help for the Allies and perhaps even interference from the civilians. Finishing the job would buy all the

Texans a ticket back to their homes, safe from the spread of Nazi poison.

Some of Sgt. Turner's buddies found a place to eat their rations among the rubble of a French village, 1945.

Taking time to eat in a French town, 1945.

CHAPTER 5

★ ★ ★ ★ ★

Germany

*Finally, my brethren, be strong in the Lord
and in the power of His might.*

Ephesians 6:10 (NKJV)

The first Texas troops walked on German soil the 19th of March, 1945. The T-Patchers quickly found an appropriate place on the monumental customs arch at Schweigen to hang the Texas Lone Star flag sent to them by Governor Coke Stevenson. The Nazis had fought to keep the Americans from crossing the river border but the 36th was now congregating on the German side after their successful first step. Before them lay the infamous Siegfried Line: an arrangement of formidable defense barriers along their border, the masterpiece of German engineers. A belt of deep anti-tank trenches, pillbox-studded hills, wire fortresses, and a pattern of pyramid shaped concrete obstacles, "dragon's teeth," constituted the bulwark of the enemy's vaunted defense.

At last poised before the Siegfried Line or Westwall, the 36th Division prepared for an assault on the Palatinate region, west of the Rhine River. The T-Patchers, not provided with armored siege guns, were expected to do little more than make a serious demonstration upon reaching the obstacle. After uncovering the Siegfried defenses, the Army planned to step in with their main effort at closer range many miles left of the Division. However, planting the Lone Star flag on the Schweigen customs house injected such an adrenalin rush, that the Texans smashed through the hard core of the Westwall, moved on to the hills in a strenuous pillbox-to-pillbox advance, and reduced the enemy's most violent opposition.[1]

Using new "beehive" explosives from the engineers, the Texans were able to clear the honeycombed hills of camouflaged pillboxes. They placed beehives alongside the doors and detonated the charge, turning the fortified box into a drum interior. Addled Germans, bleeding from their nose and ears, staggered from their holes. Prisoners were encouraged to radio their comrades of a similar fate awaiting them. Rows of white flags soon decorated the outline of the Siegfried fortress. With the vantage point of the hills taken, the valleys could be safely cleared of barriers. By the 23rd of March, Hitler's last line of defense, a once-thought impenetrable bastion, had crumbled and the Texans streamed east toward the Rhine. The 36th had accomplished what other Divisions of the 7th Army had attempted just three months earlier.

The last week of March was spent mopping up the area west of the Rhine and managing the large number of prisoners. Basically, the combat of the Division ended for the time being and a new role of governing the conquered was undertaken.[2] The Official After Action Report, 36th Division, for March 30 states, "the division was completely relieved from combat at midnight this date."[3] The Texans awoke the next morning, slowly realizing they may have fought their last great battle at the Siegfried Line. Cecil could finally write home that evening. His previous letter was penned in France while the length and outcome of the war was still quite uncertain. Rumors of the Siegfried Line caused even the most optimistic soldier to doubt a swift end to the war. Just nine days later, however, Sgt. Turner sat down to write his first letter from Germany and the war was essentially over for the 36th.

March 31, 1945
Land of the Krauts

My dear Dad & Mom,

I have time to get a few letters off now.

I have just returned from a personal appearance of Mickey Rooney. He was pretty good but needed some help to put on a show. I took two pictures of him. I hope they are good.

I am doing OK–getting a little rest. I got the pictures of the home also your letter of March 11. It looks nice. I remember it vaguely. Do you have an awning for the front porch? I really enjoyed the pictures. It is the nearest thing to actually seeing you.

Little Clay Baby is such a cute little fellow and Ava must be getting prettier every day. Why didn't someone tell me Ava was so cute! I'll start telling everyone what a cute sister I have.

Hello!–Ava and thanks to you and all for the pictures.

Love,
Cecil

Newt Turner at his home with grandson Howard Clay Boston Jr.
and daughter Ava.

Surprisingly, Deacon Turner gave his family no idea as to how the war was well in hand at this point. The average GI may not have been privilege to information concerning war status or perhaps Cecil guarded his optimism, not wanting to raise his family's hopes too soon. Only the heading, "Land of Krauts," gave the indication that the war was progressing.

The troops were getting much needed rest. Morale soared as the troops were quartered in spotless German houses. Although fraternization was still forbidden, spring sports were popular and shows more frequent. Mickey Rooney toured the area with his "Jeep Company."[4] In his journal, Cecil recorded he was at Klingenmunster when he saw the troop show. Many T-Patchers were taking advantage of a lenient leave policy and touring London and areas in France. Cecil would not go to a rest camp for another 10 days. Police action of the 36th did not require artillery radio operators. By the first of April, Sgt. Turner's radio duties were over for the time being and his journal indicates he and a buddy named Charles Ponnet were given road patrol duty at Homburg.

Cecil (left) and Charles Ponnet give the victorious #1 wave while on road patrol at Homburg.

April 3, 1945
Deep in Germany

My dear Mom & Dad,

I am doing fine as usual even tho' there have been little weather surprises. The three inches of snow have about melted now.

It hasn't been so long since I had a letter from you but I didn't get one today. There were two letters from a girl I write to in Pennsylvania. I am enclosing a money order for $100 and I may have to send some more soon and I

*don't like to carry very much around and I have about
$40 now.*

*Tell Veltie that he will be very glad to hear that I have
a German Lueger pistol and one of the famous German
P-38 pistols. I sure wouldn't take for the P-38. Best gun
made!*

*The news is good tonite. All the Italians in Northern Italy
who were fighting and all the Germans are supposed to
have surrendered. I think if the war should end I would
like to go to bed and sleep a week first.*

I think of you often.

*Love,
Cecil*

Everyday brought good news from the north—of
victories and surrenders. The end was rapidly approaching
and every morning brought the hope that this would be the
day of the final surrender of Germany. The 36th had been
given the new duty of Military Government, policing and
dealing with problems of civilian control. Most T-Patchers
were optimistic their days of facing stout, fixed German
defenses were over at last. Occupational duties brought
them face to face with the Germans who had caused the
world to go to war. The soldiers searched the bewildered
and downhearted civilians as they sifted through the rubble of their towns and lives. This "screening" was tedious
and repetitious, but infinitely better than combat.

The After Action Report, 36th Division, for April
recorded the conditions in Homburg where Sgt. Turner
was assigned:

The new area bore all the marks of recent battles and conquered populace. Many of the towns and villages, except for a few scattered suburbs, were reduced to jagged rubble heaps. The German people, plundering through their destroyed possessions, greeted the occupying troops with expressionless faces and an atmosphere of lost hope. The countryside was scarred with entrenchments, barbed wire, minefields and countless concrete casements. The valleys were dotted and torn with destroyed and abandoned equipment, and even though the war was pressed into the heart of Germany, many miles east of the Rhine, observations clearly outlined another job to be accomplished behind the lines (. . .) The mission was to occupy approximately 2,000 square miles and assist the Allied Military Government in the enforcement of military law and order, which entailed screening the civilian population, salvaging food and equipment for equal distribution, guarding military installations and maintaining motorized patrols and traffic control posts.

A systematic plan was inaugurated for the mission of occupation and the support of the military government. A mobile screening unit was set up which canvassed the sector by squares, comprehensively spot checking pedestrians, houses, refugees and transients. This unit continually picked up German prisoners of war in small outlying communities and on main routes leading through each sector. Any locality was canvassed on call at very short notice. All towns and villages were posted with military government posters and each unit fulfilled the responsibility of enforcing military laws and regulations; motorized patrols visited all the inhabited localities in the sector of responsibility at least once every 24-hour period. Check posts, open 24 hours, were established at road network centers with motorized patrols instituted between check posts.[5]

Cecil began his gun collection during "screening" duties in these German towns. All weapons were confiscated, causing quite a stockpile of munitions. The occupying troops were not to have direct dealings with the Germans other than the enforcement of the new military rules. Daily contact with the inhabitants of Nazism's homeland was difficult for many soldiers, seeing faces to blame for the hardships endured and friends killed.

April 10, 1945
Germany

Dearest Mom & Dad,

This night finds me doing alright and feeling fine. Excuse the spot on the paper for I have just had a piece of good white bread and real American butter so you can see we are doing fine and eating good.

The news is so good lately that I can't keep up with it.

We have been having a little fun lately. We rode a lot of German horses that once were used to draw artillery pieces.

It's time to go on the job so bye now.

Say hello to Ava and all.

Love,
Cecil

German towns took on a strange appearance as the troops moved into new areas. Most buildings were flying a white flag made from bed sheets and tablecloths. Village after village presented this solemn, ghost-like spectacle to conquering T-Patchers rumbling over the ancient cobblestones of the main streets. The victorious troops witnessed a white flag flying from every house and a few stunned, gloomy eyed civilians watching the parade of Allied armor. Each time a new unit entered a town, civilians were ordered confined to their homes for 48 hours. Under non-fraternization orders, the Americans ignored German wonderment and attempts at friendly conversation.[6]

After his duties at Homburg, Cecil was sent to Neustadt where his journal mentions they found "much wine." They also found horses these Texans could round up and ride, living up to their cowboy reputation.

April 11, 1945
Germany not on the front

Dearest Mom, Dad, Ava, etc,

The darkness has closed in on this part of Germany and I was out to see the sunset. Spring is here and everything is getting pretty. In another week things will all be budded out and green.

I have been doing a lot of thinking lately. This part of Germany is very pretty and I can't see why the Germans ever started a war to gain other territory.

I think I am getting a nice break in two days. I'm slated to go to Southern France.

Love,
Cecil

Deacon Turner was feeling philosophical on the evening of April 11, 1945. How he loved to be outside enjoying the beauty of God's creations. His statements about the darkness over Germany, and the oncoming of spring could be interpreted with deeper meanings. For a farm boy, he did ponder on topics way beyond machinery and weather. It made no sense to him for the greedy Germans to want more territory when theirs was a beautiful land.

Within a few days, Cecil was loaded with other T-Patchers on a boxcar bound for a rest camp on the French Riviera at Nice. Being stuffed in an old French boxcar for a 12 hour ride with little or makeshift seating was not a prelude to what was in store for these weary soldiers. After living a rather uncivilized lifestyle for two years, Cecil and the rest of these doughboys were in for a rare treat once they climbed out of their cattle car.

"I rode in this old style French railroad car for 80 miles, took about 12 hours. Paul Witheridge, Clifton Dodson"

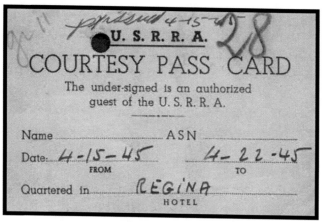

Cecil was quartered at the Regina Hotel, Nice, France, courtesy of the United States Rest and Recreation Administration during April, 1945.

April 16, 1945
In the City of Nice

Hello Mom & Dad,

Yep! Here I am on the Southern Coast of France at Nice on the Riviera. It's not so very far from the Station border. It is undoubtedly the best place for a rest camp for a soldier.

We moved up the Rhine, up on the 7th Army front, then we were relieved and occupied part of the country that we had taken. I was in charge of a motor patrol of about 18 Kilometers or about 11 miles. It was more or less traffic control and keeping the civilians in hand. We did not have a lot of trouble. We sifted every man in town one day. We call it screening.

Well, write more soon.

Love–Cecil

Sgt. Turner took the phrase "Loose lips sink ships" to heart and was rarely censored in his letters. He waited until information was no longer classified before he would disclose his position or details of his activities. More than two weeks after the 36th invaded Germany, Cecil gives his family a quick overview of their success and his new duties since the T-Patchers were relieved from combat.

This Plowboy from Roscoe had never seen anything like the French Riviera. Cecil's earlier comment about sleeping for a week could have come true if the Cote d'Azure did not offer so much: a swanky boardwalk promenade, sprawling hotels and casinos, the incomparable Mediterranean and spacious beaches. Along the Promenade Des Anglais in Nice, vacationing GI warriors found a long awaited paradise.[7]

April 17, 1945
In City of Nice

Dearest Mom & Dad, and Ava, H.C.,

My third day in Nice and I still like it here. I may send some souvenirs but everything is high priced here.

The news is good every day now. It would sure be nice if the war should end while I am here in Nice.

I came here by train from Nancy. I have enjoyed meeting different people. I've met an Austrian girl, a Russian girl, an English woman and a lot of people who speak English and make good conversation.

Have everything ready for me when I come home. Ha! Can I sleep a week?

This letter to you all. More later.

Love,
Cecil

Cecil was catching up on conversations with all kinds of people, mainly females. He was feeling like a real person again and enjoying all the sites. The Red Cross Casino Club contained an 850-seat theater and was one of the most beautiful service clubs of the war. Such a relaxed atmosphere permeated the resort, with the officers billeted in Cannes and enlisted men in Nice, that even the time-worn Army custom of saluting was discarded.[8] With all the entertainment the Riviera had to offer, just normal conversations were the highlight of Turner's day.

April 17, 1945
In City of Nice

Dearest Mom & Dad (and all relations)

I send you greetings from the people of Nice. Nice undoubtedly is the greatest resort in Europe. The American Red Cross has a building here for the enjoyment of servicemen that must have cost several million dollars. Money has always been used by the hat full here. Have my own room at Hotel.

I am forgetting the war for the time being while I am here however I hear a little news which is nearly all good.

I will be very glad to get back to the U.S. and not just because my home is there. The rest of the World may have its points but the USA can't be beaten anywhere.

I don't know how much action I'll see yet.

More letters later—Cecil

At Nice, Cecil experienced luxury he had only heard of before. The men were served their morning newspapers, if not their breakfasts, in bed. Orchestras played in the dining rooms at lunch and dinner of the better hotels. During the day, there was swimming, fishing, tennis, bicycling and roller skating to entertain as well as theaters with moving pictures in both English and French at night.[9]

The rest with no worries and responsibilities had been exactly what Cecil and the other men needed. But in the back of Sgt. Turner's mind was his desire to be home—back to the U. S., Texas, and Roscoe. At the end of the week he was ready for the trip back to Germany so his next trip would be home.

April 22, 1945
In City of Nice

Dearest Dad & Mom,

Tomorrow is my last day and my friend and I will take the train back toward the 36th Division where ever they may be. They may still be occupying part of Germany and if so, I'll go back out to an outpost somewhere and do guard duty. The Germans back behind the lines don't give much trouble. They know they have very little chance of dealing us much damage back there. We screened one town and got a small gang and their Nazi leader plus a few soldiers in civilian clothes who had jumped the front lines.

There may be a lot of mail waiting for me when I get

back. Maybe a box of candy too! I hope so anyway. How is everything in Texas now? I'm thinking of sending some of these French hairstyles home. They sure have the hair-do's! Remember me when you pray.

Love,
Cecil

We are given more details in the "screening" action Cecil had been a part of in Germany immediately following the opening of the Siegfried line. The end of March and early April must have been surreal at times. Sgt. Turner was radioing artillery strikes on March 22nd in a still uncertain war, capturing Nazi gangs hiding in surrendered villages by the first of April, then studying French hair-dos as he lounged in the Riviera by mid-April. As he contemplated return to duty, he once again reminded his parents to continue their prayer protection over him.

The day Cecil rejoined the 36th Division they were back on the offensive, moving toward the front. Men wearing the T-Patch had enjoyed their respite from battle, but some inner urge, some possible jealousy, kept gnawing at them. Colonel Vincent Lockhart expressed the feeling, "We, who had first hit the continent of Europe nearly 20 months earlier, were entitled to be in on the kill."[10]

The T-Patchers had quickly traveled 150 miles to an assembly area east of Heilbronn, preparatory to re-entering the swift-moving 7th Army line. Before the Division could collect its many units in the assembly area, the Army line had moved more than 100 miles beyond Heilbronn.[11] There is no record of who made the final decision to put the Texans back on the line. The 7th Army history merely records: "The 36th caught up with and relieved the 63rd Division at Landsberg, some 300 miles from Kaiserslauten."[12] After following and mopping up behind the fast-moving 12th Armored (a combat technique both novel and pleasant to the Texans), the 36th initiated an attack to the south from Landsberg.[13]

Braunsbach is the location Cecil listed in his journal for April 25. The next morning, just nine days before the war's end, the 36th went to bat for its final licks against the Nazis. This was fast-paced, rampaging warfare with resistance only stiffening sporadically. Units that sped forward were under the ever imminent threat of ambush by fanatical German storm troopers. Officers took few risks with their men's lives knowing the end of the war was close. To everyone but the hardcore Schutzstaffel (SS), the war *was* rapidly ending. It only took one holdout SS official in a town to lead them in a refusal to surrender. The village of Heilbronn became a tragic example. Not wanting to risk one American life, officers sent a message requesting surrender or the 36th artillery and bombers would level the city. When the SS commandant refused, civilians fled before the Army commander called for maximum support. Since targets were few and far between this late in the war, "maximum support" drew the attention of much of the Division's artillery, leading to alarming results. A few days later, the 36th drove through the rubble of the town where not a single room had four walls still standing.[14]

May 1, '45
Deep in Germany

Dearest Mom and Dad o' mine

That's a fact! I'm with the Seventh Army again and we're Deep in Germany. I'm glad to always be able to come back to the same battery. I have been in the Service for over four years and all but four days I have been in this Battery.

We have about four inches of snow this morning. Have you seen anything of Spring? How are your flowers, Mom?

I will mail another $100 money order tomorrow. I did not send one last month because I wanted to wait 'til I got paid this month and send $100 and make all the checks alike. Let me know when the check gets there dated May 2. How much will that make me—a sock full?

Dad, I have mailed a souvenir home. Have sent it to you. It's a 3-caliber rifle. Will make an excellent deer rifle. You can let Veltie take it up to his house to get it out of the way. Veltie and you can assemble it and keep it greased for me. We'll really try it out when I get home. I'm still OK and still remember where I live.

All my love,
Cecil

The day-to-day headlines in late April and early May captured the events: Berlin Falls; Munich Taken; Mussolini Executed; Himmler Makes Capitulation Move; Adolph Hitler Dies; Germans in Italy surrender.[15] The waning war was in its final countdown as the 36th speedily advanced. This was reflected in Sgt. Turner's journal as he recorded setting up the command post at Schwabmunchen on April 28th and moving it again to Weilheim in the same day. The Texans were confident they had seen the worst until they faced the blackest depth of human evil.

In their sweep southeast toward Austria, the 36th

encountered their first concentration camps. The Nazis had tucked several death camps in the southeastern corner of Germany near Dachau, Hurlach and Lansberg. Forty years later, in a conversation with his son-in-law, Cecil spoke more candidly about the discovery of these death camps. He described the day his unit moved into the area. With no clue as to what was behind the intense fortifications they were approaching, the stench caused many hardened soldiers to lose their last consumed rations. As the horror built with each step into the compound, those with stronger stomachs lost theirs as well. Cecil mentioned a pile of shoes in his notes. The scene prompted waves of images recounting innocent lives that should be walking, jumping and dancing in those shoes. The pile lay there virtually unchanged since the day they were ripped from the feet of the doomed prisoners. The bodies did not fare as well. In each concentration camp, the piles of discarded humans were in different stages of decay.

The Texans were the unfortunate ones to authenticate the unbelievable rumors of atrocities. Taking photographs of the stripped bodies, barely more than skeletons, seemed one more indignity to heap upon the stripped lives so cruelly devoured by Nazi hatred. History is grateful, however, that Sgt. Turner and other soldiers knew the importance of establishing a record of such monstrous crimes. Only when his children became adults would Cecil take the shoebox from the closet and show them the graphic images. Today, at the United States Holocaust Memorial Museum, the flag of the 36th Division, along with 34 others, is flown in honor of the concentration camp liberators.

Colonel Lockhart records in his book:

The advancing Americans were appalled at the stench of bodies, the roadside litter of dead, and the walking dead who were little more than skin stretched over bones. There was clear evidence that the SS guards, before being forced to flee, had machine-gunned their victims. In some camps, (liberated) prisoners went on the rampage, looting nearby villages, finding SS guards disguised in prison uniforms and literally tearing them to pieces upon such discovery. It became our job to restrain them. It was not a pleasant job.[16]

The fortress surrounding a concentration camp. 1945

After almost 2 years of combat, the American soldiers were still not prepared for the gruesome sights while liberating the concentration camps.

May 7, 1945
Somewhere in Austria

Dear Mom and Dad,

It's about time for breakfast but here's a short note to say hello. I mailed another gun today and I think you will get a kick out of it because you probably never saw one like it. That makes three I have sent.

News has just come that the war is supposed to be over. I sure hope it's true. Maybe I will be home by Xmas or maybe for my birthday- who knows?

I know some of you would like to know what I think of the Germans. The truth is I have not made up my mind whether all the people should be shot or just part of them. Personally, I hold the entire German nation as guilty of throwing the entire World into War and confusion. There may be some good people in Germany. I rather think that maybe there are but one can't tell who they are. They are all guilty of not stopping the Nazis instead, we are over here thousands of miles from home to do away with Nazism. The French say never trust the Germans at all.

Now that the War is about over I think we will try to have a little more recreation. Maybe go fishing now and then, etc. etc.

It looks like I stand a pretty good chance of living through this war now. How do you use a fork?

Love,
Cecil

In the remaining letters, a noticeable change in attitude toward the Germans was not surprising after Sgt. Turner witnessed the Holocaust. When any man is faced with such evil, the glimpse into depths of depravity must affect his perspective on criminals and appropriate justice. For the rest of his occupational duty, as Cecil dealt with the Germans, from former Nazis to civilians, he could not help but see the images of corpses and piles of shoes. There was no inner struggle for him to box up some guns left by the Nazis and send them home to America. If he could, he would have sent them all just to get them out of German hands. Evidently, the Army felt the same way and let the soldiers use the mail to partly dispose of the rising stockpile.

Cecil, like many other T-Patchers, began to believe he might be among the survivors of this ordeal. This brought a different kind of strain as expressed by one soldier, "those last few days, while easy as far as the fighting was concerned, were about the toughest on us. Each day you felt that if I make it today, I might end up making it. Before that, you felt that if I don't get it today, I'll get it tomorrow."[17]

The 36th was driving deeper into the narrow alpine valleys as they moved eastward toward the Austrian border. Allied strategists pointed with certainty to the mountains of Southern Germany where Hitler would gather his elite SS guard for a last stand. It was feared that from his mountain retreat, the Fuhrer might hold out for many months, possibly a year. This myth was short-lived as the 3rd and 7th Armies gave a swift left then right jab deep into the territory. The final blow came from the North as the Russians and the First Army cut off any further transfer of enemy troops. The supposedly invulnerable Inner Fortress had fallen in a clear-cut final knockout.

As the Division moved eastward in early May,

Cecil recorded engaging German stragglers in the alpine retreat of Bad Tolz. Units swept through the woods in all directions. "The big job was to screen the populace, see if villages and towns could be brought back to some kind of normal life, and meantime watch for fanatics who might snipe from any point or place."[18] In some of these elaborate homes and retreats, many T-Patchers ate their first hot meal since leaving the Rhine. There really was no front line any longer and thus no real "rear area," but that sort of action fell to part of the 36th. Policing and patrolling this sector involved several aspects: "(1) pockets of resistance, (2) concentration camps, (3) enemy equipment and supply dumps, and (4) refugee centers."[19] In addition, the 36th handled the task of corralling and transferring two trainloads of POW's and, Cecil noted in his journal, "one boatload of prisoners."

Throughout the country, many Germans were surrendering as units.

In early May, thousands of regular German soldiers, the Wehrmacht and Luftwaffe, were surrendering by company, battalion, regiment and even division. Roads were jammed with prisoners coming down out of the hills. Problems of disarming them, not to mention taking them into custody, became too time consuming.[20] Most Germans disposed of their weapons before approaching the Americans. In one spacious estate, soldiers discovered a swimming pool half-filled with weapons.[21]

This mass submission merely furnished an almost ignored background for the final days of the drive into the rotten core of the Nazis who had conquered all of Western Europe and threatened to dominate the world. SS prisoners were rarely taken. During those last days, there developed a new and acute loathing for the stupidity of the SS who fought on as Americans drove into the very heart of the Reich, making their cause utterly hopeless.[22] It was never easy to lose a comrade in arms in war, even when his end was heroic and the battle an important step in convincing the enemy of his impending defeat. But to see a buddy fall in a pointless battle cheapens his death. Colonel Lockart records the feelings of one T-Patcher:

> Our casualties in the Bavarian and Tyrolian Alps were by comparison to earlier campaigns negligible, but it was much harder to accept the fact that a screeching shell in the last minute of the war had the same lethal qualities it had in the most bitter of the early days of combat. [23]

During the sweep through the Bavarian Alps, the 36th Division arrested many high-ranking German officers. The area had been utilized for summer homes of Nazi party leaders, hospitals and rest camps for the SS. Many notorious enemy elite were captured during the last few days of the war. Reichsmarshal Herman Goering, Field Marshal Gerd von Rundstedt, and Dr. Hans Frank were three of these captives who would later face war criminal charges at the combined Allied trial at Nurnberg. Having a keen interest in the prosecution of these ruthless villains, Cecil later bought a copy of the trials when they became available on video.

The SS officers surrendered from their plush vehicles

On May 4, the 36th drove deeper into the Alpine valleys of Southern Germany and entered Austria. When the T-Patchers crossed the border, it marked the sixth country the Texans had entered. In their travel through these foreign lands, Austria stood out as the most scenic. Even in early May, massive snowdrifts still remained on the majestic Alpine peaks. There, among the vacation retreats, rumors of surrender began to circulate. Both the end to hostilities and the beauty of the Alps must have seemed unreal to the GI. His mind most certainly wandered back to months and years of death and mud.[24]

Word came down from the 7th Army Headquarters at 6:30 P. M., May 5th that signaled the end of the war. Sgt. Turner may have been on the radio the night the news came. Artillery was still clearing roadblocks and machine gun positions. A field unit captain had just requested a hit on one of these targets:

> He peered into the dusk through his glasses as the two shells whined over his head and crashed into the road block up ahead. "Deflection correct . . . 200 over . . . fire for effect." The radio crackled and he listened for the familiar "on the way," but the reply came back: "All units halt in place. Do not fire unless fired upon." The captain quietly said, "Roger . . . Roger and out . . . all right boys, pack up . . . mission complete."[25]

Even with the word coming straight from Army Headquarters, Cecil's use of the phrase, "the war is supposed to be over," in the May 7th letter may reflect the dubious feeling many doughboys reserved until more proof surfaced. That first night many of them found houses to sleep in with a few still standing guard against last minute treachery. They sat around in small groups and talked softly or not at all. One T-Patcher remembers: "I was suddenly, terribly tired. That night the battalion was the quietest I can ever remember."[26] Another Texan recalls:

> Most of us were occupied with our own thoughts and were inwardly thanking God that it was over and that there would be no groping through the early morning blackness moving up to an attack tomorrow or the next day, or the day after."[27]

Cecil mentions "pink Champaign at Kufstein" in his journal, where the Division Command Post and Rear Headquarters were located and must have celebrated the war's end. Turner felt confident enough to tell his family in essence the worst was over and he should be safe from here on. Families all over America would be reading the good news from the papers and soon in letters as well.

A lack of communication caused by the unorganized hasty retreat of the German Army prolonged the arrangements for the surrender terms. The Official After Action Report for May 8, 1945 dryly states, "Division moved into new occupational area and initiated acceptance and control of the surrender of German units in its sector."[28] Even without embellishments or exclamation points, the unemotional military report is powerful in its understatement of the importance of the day.

On May 8, in a day long convoy, T-Patchmen streamed in to accept and control the surrender and to occupy St. Johann, Kitzbuhel, and Mittersill, in the heartland of a tourist's paradise. The same day simultaneous announcements from Washington and London proclaimed the final surrender of all German forces. There in the Austrian Tyrol, the 36th realized the victory it had fought so long to achieve.[29]

Abandoned Luftwaffe planes were found scattered at the end of the war.

With the war over, a new number became the focus of every soldier's mind. The Army had developed a point system whereby each GI would be awarded increments based on months of service, overseas bonus, campaigns, etc. The number of points earned became his most vital statistic. Soldiers with the most points were the first to end their tour of duty. Cecil explained to his family the rules of this point counting game where the prize was a trip home.

May 15, 1945
Somewhere in Germany

Dear Mom and Dad,

Please say hello to everyone for me and tell them I am ok. I just don't get around to writing everybody very often. I guess you wonder when I'm going to settle down somewhere. One time I write from some country and the next time I am in another one.

This is the time I dreaded most–the time spent over here after the war is over and you just wait. We have things fixed up pretty nice tho' and it won't be so bad.

Some of you may have wondered about my number of points—well let's count them. First of all, there's 50 points for being in the Army fifty months. Then there's 25 for being overseas 25 months. Then there is 20 for the four campaign ribbons or rather campaign stars. That totals 95 points. The War Department will send me home when they can I think.

I go to bed and get lots of sleep now that there's no more radio to worry about.

Everybody be good and don't forget to mail that letter last nite!

With love,
Cecil.

One would think Sgt. Turner's letters would be more frequent with the war over. Perhaps the urgency to reassure his family of his safety was lifted or without the hours in front of the radio it was harder for Cecil to find time to write home. It is interesting Cecil used the "Somewhere in Germany" heading again, with the war over and security not a concern. Perhaps he honestly didn't know his location since he no longer had access to maps used by radio operators. However, he did occasionally have access to a typewriter because several of the letters over the remaining months were typed.

Sgt. Turner was not the only one having a hard time with boredom following VE day. There were no more complaints about sleep shortage, just the desire to be doing something worthwhile again. The average Joe could handle time away from his family and risking his life daily in order to save the world. However, keeping him so far from home in order to direct traffic or other duties even less noble, seemed a waste of time. Patience wore thin as the days clicked by, away from the life to which Cecil so desperately wanted to return.

Six impatient months with an occupational force followed hard upon winning the war in Europe. New duties and policies aimed at blotting out the Nazi mindset and helping control the economy of defeated Germany were necessary but an onerous task for the Allies. A vast horde of displaced persons became the immediate No. 1 problem of the soldier. Grumbling GI's went about their routine tasks, but not without considerable complaints and a prolonged hankering for home.[30]

Sgt. Turner gave his family a good explanation of the point system the Army used to determine which "old timers" were the next to go home. Five hundred men were sent home from the 36th Division just six days after VE Day. The number of points each man had accumulated was a topic of great importance.

The last days of field work as the troops began residing in the area towns toward the end of the war.

One of the last field meals before troops began occupying and policing German towns.

May 19, 1945
In the town of Memmingen, Germany

Dear Mom & Dad, Veltie & Doris, Ronny, etc,

The division is spread out over a large area of Germany and we are in this little town which is I guess about 75 miles west of Munich and about 150 miles east of Mulhouse, France. If you have a map, you might be able to plot where I am.

We don't have a lot to do. This morning three of us arrested two Nazis who were former SS troops. We cooperate with the Allied Military Government in every way possible. I am very interested in seeing that the bad element in Germany is stamped out.

If I ever get a good hunch on when I will be sent home I will try to write all about it. We have sent four men home since the war ended who had more points than I have. If very many men go home out of this battery I should go. But if only a few go now I will have to stay longer. The lowest man who went home had 110 points and I have 95 at present. I think I'll be coming home but just can't tell when.

Now then, Waltie Boy, I have mailed a total of 9 guns home. What do you think of that? You have never seen the likes of some of those I have sent. I have mentioned the rifle and shotgun double–barrel. The shotgun barrel has a telescopic sight and the rifle barrel has a sight of its own. The telescopic sight on the shotgun should be the very thing for getting quail on the wing. You'll see. There will be a 22 caliber single shot too. It was dangerous until I threw away the hair-trigger. Be careful with all of them and please don't let anyone get hurt. You can assemble them if you like or let them go - as you please. Some may need oiling. We'll have a time! You should have seen me open up with a shotgun the other day on a deer–no luck! Too far!

I hear that you have been working too hard again, Dad, and I don't know what I'll ever do about it.

I sincerely hope you are feeling better, Mom, and maybe you are by now.

Thanks for writing Doris. I received the letter you wrote while Veltie was planting. You can tell Ronny that every letter I write is for him. Ha!

How are you, Ava. I know you will be reading this too so, Hello!

My main worry now is I might happen to get home about the time cotton is opening! Somebody might hand me a cotton sack when I get off the train. Ha! That's all folks!

Can I come home now?

Love,
Cecil

Cecil in one of Germany's occupied towns. 1945

Cecil (left) and buddies finding a place to cook in a
war-torn German town. 1945

Cecil's last letters from occupied Germany did not have descriptions of church services like there had been in the early months of the war. Perhaps there were infrequent opportunities for Army group worship or he stopped including them in his letters for some reason. Evidence suggests he was still going to church, even though he did not mention it in his letters. While occupying Germany, he had the opportunity to attend local church services with the townspeople. Cecil did refer to some of the local churches in his journal during this period and brought home a memento from one. Somehow he obtained the original or copy of the following sermon on onion skin paper. Perhaps the pastor wanted the occupational forces to know what was being said and handed out copies in English. It is possible Rev. Asmussen delivered the message in English for the visiting troops to get the full impact of his sermon. Cecil would refer to the pastor's statements years later when teaching in his home church. The sermon was indeed worth holding onto for many generations to come. Turner handwrote the heading:

Service in German Church: Hall,
Germany right after the war.
The following sermon was delivered
May 20, 1945
by Rev. Hans Asmussen at Hall, Germany.

Scripture: Deuteronomy 28:1–6 and 15–19 [KJV]

And it shall come to pass, if thou shalt harken diligently unto the voice of the Lord thy God, to observe and to do all his commandments which I command thee this day, that the Lord thy God will set thee on high above all nations of the earth: And all these blessings shall come on thee, and overtake thee, if thou shalt harken unto the voice of the Lord thy God. Blessed shall the fruit of thy body, and the fruit of thy ground, and the fruit of thy cattle, the increase of thy [herds], and the flocks of thy sheep. Blessed shall be thy basket and thy store. Blessed shalt thou be when thou goest out. But it shall come to pass, if thou wilt not harken unto the voice of the Lord thy God, to observe to do all his commandments and his statutes which I command thee this day; that all these curses shall come upon thee, and over take thee: Cursed shalt thou be in the city, and cursed shalt thou be in the field. Cursed shall be thy basket and thy store. Cursed shall be the fruit of thy body, and the fruit of thy land, the increase of thy [herd], and the flocks of thy sheep. Cursed shalt thou be when thou comest in, and cursed shalt thou be when thou goest out.

We stand today before the ruins of our cities. What formerly required centuries, has taken place before our very eyes in two years. Giant cities have become rubble.

We stand before the graves of those killed in air raids. Their number is still beyond calculation.

We stand at the end of a thousand years of history which was delivered to us as a heritage of pride and before us we can see no possible way of its continuation.

We stand before the wreckage of a great flowering industry and it is becoming evident that unimaginable misery and poverty is about to overwhelm us.

The greatest war in the history of the world has come to an end. In spite of fabulous accomplishments, we have been defeated in disgrace and shame.

We think of our war dead. Our hearts contract when it becomes clear to us what result follows their efforts and their sacrifices.

We pity the incalculable numbers of maimed. We cannot hide from our eyes the burdensome life that awaits them.

Only few of us understand the flood of misery that gushes forth from concentration camps, prisons, correction houses and threatens to engulf and drown us.

Our faith in humanity has been shattered. Our faith in promises has been broken. Our faith in ideals has been desecrated.

Men have forgotten how to pray. The path to the church has been practically blocked for the whole nation.

We now stand before a great void. Such is the situation that all realists must see.

It is terrible that we find it impossible to escape or suppress the question of guilt. How much we would prefer that we knew nothing of all this and could start again anew. But the world grants us no rest, she screams at us with the question of guilt, and whether we will or not, we must answer our own nation, and we must answer the whole world. One can well understand when no one dares attempt to answer. For that reason it is necessary for the church to step into the breach and today we shall offer a contributor on this question.

The church is to blame, the church of both confessions. Our guilt stretches far into the past. Our guilt lies in the fact that we have remained silent where we should have spoken out, and spoken up when we should have suffered in silence. For long decades we have tried to practice a philosophy of life which had no word of final truth. Instead of saying definitely "No," we have said "Yes, but." We have been indifferent to the rock of our salvation and the treasures of our truth—namely, the Word of God. We have striven with each other when we should have been unified. We have debated when we should have prayed. We have practiced no discipline when we should have banished all sin. We have often failed to withstand when we should have stood firmly with body and soul and sacrificed our very lives if necessary. We have pushed ourselves forward in mock importance when we should have silently suffered persecution. We have allowed ourselves to be pushed into a corner when we should have cried aloud openly.

All this makes our guilt plain in spite of the persecution which the grace of God has granted the church to endure in these last years.

The German citizen is guilty. That citizen is guilty who in all situations desired to be left alone. That citizen is guilty who in his desire for security surrendered justice and righteousness. Guilty is the citizen who was willing to remain silent about all atrocities far into the war, so long as military success was obtained. Guilty is the citizen to whom victory became a God. Guilty is the citizen who has allowed the regime to influence and control his soul when such influence dare never have granted to anyone except Almighty God. Guilty is the citizen who consented to the suppression of all truth in his own heart. Yes, we are all guilty, great and small, rich and poor, educated and uneducated. Destitution, poverty, misery and war have not come upon us without cause. German obeisance must plead guilty.

Something should be said about the guilt of our soldiers, but because they are not here to defend themselves we will pass up that question for the time being.

Nevertheless, a word must be said concerning the Party. Its leaders are not beyond my reach, but I have spoken to them so openly that no doubt can remain as to our explicit understanding of each other. Therefore I must be permitted to speak today to the followers though the leaders are no longer here. The party has lied to us from the beginning and has done so knowingly. The party has devoured our wealth and has thereby fattened itself. The Party has trampled the self-respect of mankind into the dust in its newspapers. The Party has lead the German people astray and betrayed them to the lowest levels of tale bearing to the degree that even in the occupation it continues. The Party has destroyed justice. The Party has robbed the freedom of millions of people. The Party has started this war. The Party has robbed us of the flower of our youth. For 12 years the Party has murdered a million human beings each year in concentration camps and executions. The Party has not only sacrificed and exposed our fatherland to destruction to the last moment, but also destroyed much with its own hands.

All this demands justice. There must be expiation. We have no grounds for complaint when the occupation forces demand expiation. The German people will perhaps be required to atone beyond what seems reasonable to us. For all unatoned wrong often drags on for centuries. Therefore we dare not resist the arm of justice; especially since we would not resist injustice. Fortunate indeed is he whom God does not require to take part in action of atonement and revenge. It is the lot of us all that with every stroke of the sword of justice which now falls upon us, we cower in alarm and penitence. For there is no doubt that seldom or perhaps never in history has the punishment of crime been so obvious and so terrible as we see it at present. Only God has the right to check or stop this righteous judgment.

It is our duty to sever all connections with the Party both in letter and in spirit. We must say to the nations and we can say it with justice that the Party is not the German people. They will not believe us and rightly they can not believe us if we do not show them proof of the fact that we do not have, and do not wish to have any connections with the Party whatsoever. Here everyone is called to work together, whether he was a Party member or not; to sever all relations. But do not suppose that this will be an easy task. The problem is not solved by merely hating and despising Party members individually or collectively. We must, to be sure, hate and despise the sin itself that has been committed, but we must seek to win the sinner. It is a dangerous thing to seek to contribute to the judgment of God.

You say you do not know of all this ruthless cruelty. That is only partly true. There are hardly any German people who had not intimations. The City of Hall knew at least this, that before their gates political prisoners were tortured and starved. So everyone either knew or suspected one or another of the many inhuman practices taking place in the name of the German people.

You say you could not have changed matters. It is true that every murmur or shrug of the shoulder carried a death penalty when noticed. But the question remains, had we resisted in the beginning as strongly as possible, could such things have come to pass? The question is whether we did not close our eyes because of convenience? The question is whether we did not by our very silence from the beginning encourage these arch criminals in the crimes?

I will tell you one thing—we have seen the devil at work as he has enslaved mankind. This is not justification for us, but it is the only adequate explanation for what we have gone through. We have been the victims of a fearful nightmare for 12 years, and we are now awakening. God has allowed us our heart's desire. He has demonstrated before our very eyes that the doctrine that man has complete freedom of choice, is a great swindle.

Now we see in what bonds we have nearly been strangled. What shall become of us? The devil will whisper in our ears that this is time for despair. That has also already been told us by those who until now are in power, and how in self-righteous cowardice have fled.

But God tells us it is a time to repent. It shall not be preached in vain, that God gave His Son into the world in order that we might live through Him. Jesus Christ has saved us from condemnation, because He took our iniquities upon Himself; and this shall not be preached in vain.

So let us turn again to God. Perhaps his great wrath that has broken out will be stilled. Perhaps we can find our way to God's heart in which we can come to the day of judgment, wrapped in mercy for Christ's sake.

But it will be necessary that we will all actually turn to Him. That will be a great and difficult step. He who takes it must transform his life completely and tread a new path with caution.

Therefore let no one believe he can deceive God. All who now find their way to the church shall carefully consider what they are doing. God is a jealous God who will not tolerate shame.

We ministers stand before an enormous responsibility. We must not only preach to you and preach in an entirely new way; we must first and above all represent you and defend you before God, which is our most difficult task.

If we become really devout, there is yet hope. Then the Lord will again let the light of His goodness and mercy shine upon us. Then He will repent of His judgment which He has visited upon mankind.

And now I must say a word about the foreign nations. Let no one be deluded that it will help us in the hour to call to the attention of the foreign nations their guilt in this matter. I earnestly beg you not to be disturbed by the humiliating things we must endure or to think that they are no better than we. We are not the judges of the nations. At this time God has seen fit to make them our judges. It is now especially important that we accept the judgment that has come over us. We must now confess before God from the depths of our souls, that if worse judgment were heaped upon us, we still would have no right to complain.

It is also necessary that in this hour which God has given us, a word must also be spoken to the foreign nations. The church has already begun to speak to them. We will not cease to do so at all times and to plead for you all. But if these pleas are to have any success, they must be presented in the right way. We must await the hour when we can properly present it. We must find a medium in which we can meet them on equal terms. Our armor has been defeated. Our propaganda has harmed us more than all lost battles. Our crimes have made us a disgrace before the whole world. Yes, my listeners, would that our penitence before God, and would a new opportunity according to God's laws be given us that we might rise above all the nations of the world as an example of true piety. That would really be the only chance that we now have, and it would be an opportunity of honor. It would win for us the respect of all to whom God and eternity are important. To such a pathway I call all my brother ministers, as far as my voice reaches. I cry out to all the churches as far as God allows me to preach. The worldly wise of our people have become a disgrace in their wisdom. I do not doubt that God is ready to demonstrate His truth through us, that the foolish in God have greater wisdom than the wise of the world, and now let me again read to you the beginning of our text: - Deut. 28:1–5

'And it shall come to pass, if thou shalt hearken diligently unto the voice of the Lord thy God, to observe and to do all his commandments which I command thee this day, that the Lord thy God will set thee on high above all nations of the earth: And all these blessings shall come on thee, and overtake thee, if thou shalt hearken unto the voice of the Lord thy God. Blessed shalt thou be in the city, and blessed shalt thou be in the field. Blessed shall be the fruit of thy body, and the fruit of thy ground, and the fruit of thy cattle, the increase of thy [herd], and the flocks of thy sheep. Blessed shall be thy basket and thy store. Blessed shalt thou be when thou comest in, and blessed shalt though be when though goest out.'

"Therefore we dare not resist the arm of justice; especially since we would not resist injustice." The pastor presented a bold message addressing all factions entangled in the unholy mess. The sermon helped Cecil solidify his own judgments on the German people he faced daily during the tense occupational relationship.

Sgt. Turner stayed at Memmingen for the next month carrying out his policing duties. According to the official records, all of the 36th Artillery units were assigned to this area. Even though he said there was little to do, his group uncovered SS troops hiding in the area as late as the 15th of May.

Cecil sends photo home of walking the streets in occupied Germany.

Cecil (left) and friends in a German occupied town. 1945

Police work involved enforcing laws governing civilians. The sign tells the German civilians they are forbidden past this point.

The Army and the Red Cross tried to appease and compensate the soldier by providing clean German houses for the troops and familiar amenities. Even with the nightclubs, baseball diamonds and theaters, the veteran combat soldier deplored his "country club" existence and the static duties of occupation compared to the dutiful sense of accomplishment which had consumed his life for the past two years.

May 28, 1945
Memmingen, Germany

Dear Mom and Dad,

I received your letter of May 16 yesterday and I am glad once again to hear that you are all alright. It was the first time you had not mentioned being in bed so you are probably fit and well now.

At present I have no news for you on when I will be home. I will probably get an additional five points which will make me one hundred even. The next bunch slated to leave in four days have 102 and at present I have 95. That might give some idea. I should get a discharge but of course I do not know.

Dad, I will make a real effort to get you a pistol and bring it home to you. It is a little late now but maybe so yet. Say, Dad, I am really proud of my collection of guns and I hope all of them get there. I know I have mailed nine of them to you but it may be ten I am not sure. I hope it is not too much trouble to go to the depot so often. I hope it is years and years before the Germans are allowed to even have a 22 rifle again.

I am very sorry to hear that the wheat might fall short but I have one consolation–it always fools you one way or the other and it usually makes more than we think it will. Who has a combine now?

Just a minute the mail has just come in and I had a letter from Veltie.

I was mistaken. The letter was from you written on the 18th. All were well and you told me all about what happened on Mother's Day. Yes, I could smell the perfume or sachet I believe you called it.

Now that it did not arrive on time, I may as well tell you that you were supposed to have gotten a pillow on or about Mother's Day. I hear that most of the other boys had the same luck though. It may have arrived by now. I sent it for both Mother's and Father's Day. Nothing has ever been right the last four years so I guess I can just wait till it arrives.

Perhaps I will have a gun for Wade when I get home. I do not think that you should look for any of them until about the time this letter gets there. I sure will be glad to hear that all of them have arrived.

That is about all for tonite.

All my love,
Cecil

Cecil (right) and friend on German streets. Sign shows the T-Patchers where to pick up their mail. (during occupational period in 1945)

Sgt. Turner was still counting points like every other soldier. He was getting close to the magic 100 which would be a ticket home on the next transport. His impatience was already showing as the late arrival of his Mother's Day gift was added to a military complaint list he had mentally compiled over the past four years. For soldiers whose days had been packed with action for several years, it is understandable for these occupational days to drag. Cecil, the usual optimist, was showing signs of stress. It seems ironic that his stress surfaced while in relative safety compared to the unsure chaos he had lived through the previous two years.

(typed)

June 1, 1945
Memmingen, Germany

Dear Mom, Dad, Ava, and all,

Evidently the mail is not getting home as fast as it is getting over here as your letter of May 25th came yesterday but you had not heard from me since VE Day.

Naturally I am OK and feeling fine as usual.

I saw four of the fellows of my battery off today for home. That leaves 19 men ahead of me in my battery. Those men are the fellows who are sporting 96, 97, 98, 99, or 100 points. They were in the Army in the Fall and I came in the Spring, in March.

Sometime ago I took several rolls of pictures and here's some of them. A great number of them I will like to keep as souvenirs for myself so pass them on to Veltie as he has quite a number already he is keeping for me.

Since you have written that Wade also has a collection of guns I will make an effort to find more guns and maybe I can give him some when I get home.

Love,
Cecil

The occupational forces must have rounded up most of the guns in the first month. It became harder to locate any to send home. As Martha had been so good to write over the past three years, Cecil wanted to do something nice for his stepmother's son, Wade.

There were not as many requests for prayer as there were back in the heat of battle. At this stage of the war, Sgt. Turner seemed to be like so many of us, presuming capability of handling things after the crisis period is past. Perhaps this is also the reason the remaining time overseas was difficult to tolerate since he was trying to "handle" everything on his own. Souvenirs in his war memorabilia indicate Deacon Turner was still faithful in church attendance, however, with services held on a regular basis in the German towns. The chaplains did their best to see to the spiritual need of their troops. Cecil had mentioned a Baptist chaplain earlier in the war and may have been referring to Lieutenant Colonel Herbert E. MacCombie who was head of 36th Division chaplains.

Chaplain MacCombie had a similar attitude toward the Germans as Cecil was reflecting in his letters to family in Roscoe. MacCombie's opinions may have been a byproduct of the hundreds of burials he had officiated the past two years. He tells of two encounters with the Germans during occupation that emphasize the typical relationship between the occupational forces and the local civilians. He was helping with a displaced persons camp with 175 French, Dutch, Polish and Russian men and women needing food and shelter. When the local Burgomeister was not interested in helping, the chaplain informed him,

'I will go to your house and take out all the food there. Then I will go to the next house, and the next . . . ' The Burgomeister capitulated and the displaced persons were fed. In providing housing, a similar scenario developed, and again the Chaplain had to threaten to put them all in the Burgomeister's house. A hospital suddenly came to mind whereupon the Chaplain once again faced an arrogant administrator. She haughtily informed him that her beds were clean and these dirty women would not be allowed to spoil them. With new grit developing after each cavalier attitude, MacCombie told the smug manager, 'It makes no difference to me where you Germans sleep. You can sleep on the ground, if necessary. Tonight these women will sleep in beds. That is an order!' [31]

A similar prejudice was encountered when the chaplains tried to provide for the Jewish troops during Passover. They once again went to a city official to inquire as to the location of the town synagogue. He replied, "We burned it to the ground. There is no place for Jews here." [6] Chaplain MacCombie had noticed a strong reaction when he used the German word "mussen," and discovered that its meaning was stronger than the textbook translation of "must." The chaplain used the word "mussen" a few times that day and miraculously a local theater became available. It was also cleaned and prepared by the begrudging local Germans. The chaplain records in his journal:

We held our Passover. We had set 200 places. When General John E. Dahlquist arrived with his aide, we had 201 men present, but we managed another place. It was the first Seder Feast there since Hitler had come to power. Perhaps it was the first in all Germany. General Dahlquist made an appropriate address (. . .) [and] the men seemed to thoroughly enjoy the occasion. When the party was over, several men came to me and offered to help clean up the place. I told them, 'that will not be necessary. This time the Germans will clean up after you.' The Germans did. They now understood my 'mussen.' [32]

June 5, 1945
Memmingen, Germany

My dear Mom and Dad,

I don't have any letters to answer so I will just have to try to create something to write about.

I went fishing today and enjoyed it however I just got one nibble. You can't eat nibbles tho'! It was the first time I ever fished for trout. They won't bite anything unless it's alive and moving so it's a little different from our fishing. I saw one fish that must have been two feet long. I think if I had hooked him I would have dived in after him. There was a spot where the trees grew out over the creek and the underbrush was thick. I could sit there and watch the fish below. I would drop my hook down among the fish and they would look it over good. It seems they would all go over to one side and talk it over. They would agree not to have anything to do with that American and his hook. We had salmon for supper. Ha!

Just for luck I will list the guns I have sent home so you will know when they arrive which ones they are. You could for instance say that the shotgun with the peep-sight has arrived.

The guns are: 3 German military bolt action rifles—31 caliber—model 98, I believe.

1 shotgun and rifle combination with a telescopic sight.

1 large caliber rifle—looks like buffalo gun, has large peel sight.

1 22 caliber rifle single shot–not worth much–

1 22 caliber bolt action rifle–heavy

1 French bolt-action rifle–military-

1 British military rifle–bolt action

1 lever action large Cal. Rifle–old gun

1 shotgun and rifle combination–regular sight

1 real old Boar gun–shoots darts instead of ammunition. Made to kill wild boar

1 Belgian bolt-action military rifle–short gun and nice deer gun.

Also 4–German flare pistols. They are made to shoot flares at night. Don't let anyone shoot shotgun shells in them– might blow up!

Gee! That's 13 rifles–what a collection!

There's nothing new about my coming home yet. I might write a little more but it's 12:15 and I'm sleepy.

Love,
Cecil

Composing the in-depth description of his German fishing adventure was fun for his family to read and picture. There must have been more men than work for Cecil to spend such a leisurely afternoon coaxing those trout to his hook.

The complete list of guns shows quite a variety and would be a curiosity to his family familiar only with the common shotgun or rifle. Not too many flare guns were used on cotton farms in Roscoe, Texas. He knew they would enjoy such novelties; and a gun collection was the perfect souvenir for a returning veteran. Cecil was glad to take them far from the bloody hands that had used them as instruments of evil against the innocent.

June 16, 1945
Laupheim, Germany

Dearest Mom and Dad,

Your letters of June 4ᵗʰ and 8ᵗʰ got here today and I'm glad everything was alright with you.

The next day-

Your letter of June 10ᵗʰ came today and it sure is nice to be getting mail again. There was a period there that had made me a little worried.

I don't know if it would be possible to find silverware or not. Do you need it or were you thinking of what I might need some day. Let me know just in case I see something. What is a set worth with a nice design–sterling? I might could buy you a set or maybe one for myself too or maybe I won't even see any at all.

I'm certainly glad that the material I wrapped the gun was useful to you. It came out of a Nazis wrecked house and I don't know whether it was a tablecloth or what. Anyway, I'm glad someone will get some good use out of it. I wish I could send you a lot of the things the Nazis have robbed the World of.

It's good news to hear that the first gun has gotten there. I'm not sure which one it is. If it has a chip off part of the stock it must be a rifle.

I'm sending a few more pictures you can pass on to Veltie and he will be glad to see them too. He has a great number he's keeping for me. They are mostly souvenir photos I want to keep.

I must go wake up the guards.

Love and goodnight,
Cecil

It had taken a month to get a postal problem sorted out after VE Day and mail flowing to the Division's new location. The Texas Artillery Unit was relieved from the Memmingen area by elements of the 80th Infantry Division. The 36th Division Official After Action Report for June 13th, 1945 also indicates that one artillery battery and the Division Command Post moved on to Laupheim. Cecil would be there a few weeks before the next assignment.

The Turners must have been like every other family in the world: using the phrase, "while you are there . . ." as a prelude to pick up something for them. If items were not free, as in the case of confiscated guns, no bargains could be found with the inflated prices from the local merchants who were targeting these Americans with money in their pockets.

There is a hint that Cecil must be pulling some guard duty these days since he ends the letter by needing to go wake someone, presumably, for the next shift.

Otherwise, he did not give us much of an idea what his duties entailed in the previous month.

June 25, 1945
(on Hotel Post, Laupheim stationery)

Dearest Mom and Dad,

Your letter of June 18ᵗʰ I received today and you had been feeling bad because you worked too hard canning peaches. Dad has finished counting his Father's Day gifts.

Don't let that news article worry you too much about the 36ᵗʰ being occupational troops. The Division may stay over here, but I will come home as soon as there's shipping. I'm an old timer—100 points!

I have lost much of my ability to write that I once had but I will try to describe them. The Germans are generally obedient and meek. They cooperate with us. They want to be friendly but under the Allied regulations, our orders are not to even have the least thing to do with them. There are those who are permitted to deal with them for all of us. For instance, one of our boys speaks German well so he takes all of our laundry to a place and they do a pretty good job. The Germans all work hard and manage well. The entire family works and even the old people do a lot of work. They are thrifty and fairly clean. I believe I can say that most of the Germans where I have been like Americans. Everyone likes Americans. Americans are different and they are liked the World over except those who might be jealous. The Germans, a lot of them, like us better than they like their own soldiers.

I have been speaking of the common ordinary German

who might be walking past the hotel right this minute. Then there are those who are directly responsible for the war. You see the hate in their eyes when we pass them. If they are the right age and physically fit, they were in the SS troops. They are cruel and brutal and are guilty of every crime in the books. The ordinary Germans, some of them, agree that SS troopers should be shot. The Germans who caused the war are generally considered to be the Prussians or the Junkers. I have not been that far up north into Germany but for hundreds of years the Prussians have tried to force the rest of Germany to be part of their military machine so they could conquer the world. This time they almost did it! Please don't misunderstand me. I am not in sympathy with any German but there are those who are directly responsible for the war and those who are indirectly responsible. They are all guilty of not opposing the Nazi party and Hitler and what he stood for. In the last election, Hitler was the German choice by the vote of the people. The Nazi party beat the Socialist party. There are a lot of people who think they are the super-race and will always think so. We have the vicious men and women in prison. My idea is to kill all war criminals and completely disarm Germany forever and control it for a long period. The schools should be supervised for two generations.

More later-
Love, Cecil

Don't know when I'll be home yet!

You forgot to write the last time-Dad

C.T.

It sounds as if both Martha and Newt were like many of their generation who would work until they were ill. That was the way it was in their day. Folks didn't just sit around when there was work to be done—and there was always work to be done.

Newt was worried when he read that the 36th was being listed in the permanent occupational force to take over in July. Cecil reassured his father this would not affect the "old-timers" from being sent home. Fifteen hundred more from his Division had been sent home that month. With the magic 100 points needed, Cecil was sure he would be among the next group to go.

Sitting at the hotel where he was probably quartered while in Laupheim, Cecil gave a brief history lesson and concise analysis of the German people. He had seen Red Cross personnel and trucks fired upon, slaughtered horses, burned French homes, and finally, inhuman capability in the attempted extinction of a race. In the Alps, he had also viewed the bloated lifestyle of the Nazi elite. Having lived among them for several months now, he tried to put the puzzle pieces together as to how this German enigma reared up in the middle of Europe.

Sgt. Turner also had some definite opinions as to the policies concerning the future of Germany. His letter almost sounds like a political platform stated before an election: the execution of war criminals, complete disarmament, and supervision of future generations.

June 29, 1945
Landa, Germany

Dearest Mom and Dad,

I have made a little shift in location and am now with the 63rd Infantry Division instead of the 36th Inf. Div. The divisions are organized exactly the same way and I am with the corresponding battery in this division. I think I will like it alright here. It won't be much different here. The food is ok. I left the old battery yesterday that I had been with for four years and got here today.

This immediate sector is sure rich (the soil). Just outside our window there are vegetables galore- lettuce, collards, raspberries, strawberries, onions, pears, cabbage, etc.

Say, Dad, I have mailed a radio home for my souvenir. It is an eleven tube short-wave German Navy radio. I mailed it in two packages because it was too heavy to send in one box (70 pound limit). I plan to have it converted when I get back to use American tubes. It may be worth about 200 dollars. You can open it if you care to but watch out for all the parts that are loose in one of the boxes. I wrapped the tubes well. It might not get there but I wanted to try to get it through. If it's in the way have Veltie take it up to his house. Tell Veltie all about it and tell him we should be able to tune half-way around the world with that set. It will require work done on it, which I will have done in Breckenridge. I also mailed two meters home that may be valuable. They test voltage amps and mil-amps. I have some ideas on what to do with all of the stuff.

I also mailed a double barreled muzzle loading pistol home for a souvenir and a package of pictures (Kodak) and some papers I want to keep.

Will let you know if I hear anymore about coming home.

Much love,
Cecil

The Pictorial History of the 36th Division records a change in the Division that Cecil was a part of that summer. "Before V-J Day, the Division had been listed as a part of the permanent occupation force and an exchange of personnel with the 63rd Infantry and the 12th Armored Division took place to start old-timers on their way."[33] It seems the Army was reorganizing in order to get those with the most points home first. Sgt. Turner was not thrilled to be leaving the Texas Division but was going to make the best of what he hoped was a short situation.

Since Roscoe was a small town, Newt Turner was well acquainted with the local postmaster. After all thirteen guns and then the radio passed through the post office, they became best friends, spending time together almost every day. There must have been questions like, "OK, now what is Cecil going to do with a flare gun?" or "Where is he going to shoot a boar in Nolan County?" The last package must have prompted another query: "A German radio? Who is he going to call in Germany?"

July 2, 1945
Landa, Germany

Dearest Mom and Dad,

I'm sorry if you haven't been getting all of my mail. I don't get very much mail but I always write more letters than I receive. This is my second v-mail tonite. Tell Mrs. Haney that the best camera I could find would cost about $800 and that all good cameras are selling at a premium. I might be able to buy her a 35-millimeter German camera for $100 but I don't know. I have seen some of the best cameras in the world over here but I don't think she would want me to try to buy her one since the soldiers have run the price up so high. The silverware purchase is *almost hopeless too.*

I don't like to hear that you and Dad have been working too hard. Dad, I know how it is. You try to farm a little and get too much and Mom tries to can up fruit etc. and puts herself in bed. Guess I can't prevent that but I hate to hear of it. Tell everyone hello and that I'm plenty tired of Germany. I had a long talk with Wallace. He is also with the 63rd Div.

All my love,
Cecil

Sgt. Turner's move to Landa would be his last before his transfer home. He had time to get to know the area very well in the two months he was stationed there. Farm boy Cecil was impressed with the rich soil and the plentiful gardens.

Cecil must have convinced his family no bargains were available in 1945 in occupied Germany. No more inquiries were made about purchases for people before he came home. He could not convince them to take it easy, however, and Deacon Turner could do nothing to lighten the load until he was home again. He had seen enough of Germany and was ready for the flatlands of Roscoe.

July 12, 1945
Landa, Germany

Dearest Mom and Dad,

I received your letter of July 5th today and that's not so bad (7 days) even tho' it did go through the 36th Division first.

Everyday seems to bring me a little closer home but I still have nothing definite. One of my old pals of four years standing goes home tomorrow. He has 101 and I have 100.

Say, Dad, it was about time you were writing again. I guess I will have to forgive you now that you wrote that last letter. Maybe you had better not expect me back exactly the same as I was but I'm not a nervous wreck. You said that some of the boys were nervous that came home from the war. You may not notice the change in me so much, however it has been a war of nerves. I feel like I need a rest somewhere at a quiet place with not a care in the world.

One more gun makes 11. That's all but four. Maybe all will soon arrive. I want to see those things. What a mess of guns!

I will get some sleep now.

I hope to hear from you again soon and hope to be in the good ole U.S. before too long.

Love,
Cecil

The wear and strain of war never showed on Cecil like others that returned from combat. He was somehow able to deal with all he saw and trust the Lord to protect him from the bullets that ravage the body and also the ones that damage the spirit and soul. Many years later, in his spiritual journal, Cecil would write:

'And be not conformed to this world: but be ye transformed by the renewing of your mind, that ye may prove what is that good, and acceptable, and perfect, will of God.' Romans 12:2 (KJV)

To what extent do you have the thoughts of Christ? To that same extent you have the power of Christ. Do we believe that this omnipotent, omnipresent, unchangeable Christ, our redeemer God—will walk with us all day and cause us to feel his Holy Presence?

Do we think this is too much to venture?

Do we think we are sticking our neck out?

Remember: 'Lo, I am *with* you always,'—all day, every day.

God had been with him and guided his mind and guarded his life. After two years of apprehensive living in constant vigilant observation, it would take some time to completely relax.

July 23,1945
Landa, Germany

Dearest Mom and Dad, Ava, Cassie, Auti, Agnes, etc, etc,

How are you today? I am fine. This is Sunday and a pretty one too. I went to church this morning. As you know you don't go to different denominational churches in the Army. It's either Catholic or Protestant. I enjoyed the singing more than anything and a fellow sang a solo and he has a very nice voice. I suppose it was a Lutheran Church building. There was an organ and some fellow had to pump the bellows while another fellow played it.

I'm sorry I can't get Mrs. Haney a camera. It would give me great pleasure to be able to get her one. No doubt they are the best in the world (German).

Speaking of getting me a car. I don't know what to tell you. Do you mean Wade might be able to get a new '42 model? Whatever is best you can do for me. I leave anything of that nature (business nature) up to a "committee" of Dad, Hubert, Veltie and not burden anyone else. Ha!

Say! If I can get me an Army jeep worth the money when I get out then I would sure consider it. I wouldn't pay what some civilians have already paid. They cost the Army more than $1300 new. Some civilians have paid about $700 to $800 for reconditioned ones resold from the Army. If you don't know what a jeep is good for I'll tell you when I get home. Don't let them fool you in alright. They weigh about the same as a Ford automobile.

12 guns so far–only 3 more to go! Watch for the other boxes. 4 flare–pistols–sword–pictures, etc, etc.

How are all of you? I should write to you more, Auti, Agnes, and Cassie, but I just can't. I manage to write once in awhile to Ava–or answer part of her letters. Remember I love you tho'!

Dad, I wish I could tell you when I'll be home but I just can't tell yet. I wouldn't say this to just anyone but I know you won't worry since the War is over. I am plenty fed up with four years of this stuff. If you ever see any articles written by Bill Mauldin you will know what I mean. He draws all of the cartoons headed UP FRONT or SWEATIN' IT OUT. He also wrote a book. There isn't much democracy in the Army. Don't ever vote for someone for office because he was an officer in the Army.

I never have to work anymore—eat, sleep, talk, sunbathe, etc.

I'll go to bed now.

Your far-a-way son,
Cecil

While occupying Germany, the chaplains used the local churches for their services. It would be interesting to know if most German villages continued using their church buildings during the months while sharing their facilities with the Americans. Cecil always loved singing and the musical part of worship was one of his favorite parts.

Evidently, Cecil's dad and brothers were working out a plan to have a car waiting for him when he arrived. Just the discussion of the possibility sounded good to him. To be a civilian, driving around as he pleased would be a dream come true. One military influence showed in his favorable opinion of the Army jeep. He was not too impressed with most other aspects of military, including the lack of democracy. He never spoke ill of any particular officer and even praised a few—following their careers in the newspapers after the war. However, his warning about criteria for electing officials leaves little doubt concerning his opinion of Army officers in general and may offend some, but it is humorous to most of us.

July 29, 1945
Landa, Germany

Dearest Mom and Dad,

Your letter of July 18 came today and I was very glad to hear the news again.

Your address was wrong but it came because the APO was correct. It's 63rd Div.

It looks like I'm not going to make it home for my birthday. At one time I will be optimistic and think I'll be home in a few weeks but right now I don't know. I just don't know! It's a slow process.

Say, Dad, I understand why the Germans are so hard to whip. They are such hard workers. They can turn out plenty of work with their little ole carts, rakes, mowers, scythes, ox plows, one-horse binders, etc. They have some of the prettiest truck farms here I ever saw. I am going to try to get home with some tomato seed that I hope will grow in the Divide. It's a cross between a regular tomato and a climbing tomato. The tomatoes are in clusters and plenty of them.

I will write as soon as I get anything definite on when I'm coming home.

I do nothing but eat and sleep. Guess I will be lazy when I get home. There's not a thing to write. I'm still just "sweating it out" over here waiting for something to happen.

Love,
Cecil

During the four years he was in the Army, the two divisions Cecil was assigned to used the same two numbers in reverse order. (36th → 63rd — what are the chances?) It was confusing to his family and delayed his mail service at times.

Sgt. Turner was anxious for something to do but

did enjoy watching the farmers in their work. He would have enjoyed visiting them and helping if they were still in France. The non-fraternization rules kept him from getting to know the hardworking families he watched. The work ethic of the farmers was the only positive statement made about these people he lived among for several months.

July "32" 1945 (Aug. 1ˢᵗ)
Landa, Germany

Dearest Mom and Dad,

I'm not in much mood to write but maybe you would like to hear anyway. This is Wednesday nite about dark. It's been a little cool for two days after a rain here. The mud here is just about like it is at Roscoe - black and sticky. The fruits and vegetables are coming into their own now. I went out and inspected a little patch of sweet corn today. I'm keeping an eye on it and some night we'll have roasting ears for supper.

I've seen some odd things here. There are apples that grow on vines up on a tall fence. There's a rose tree about 7 feet tall. Their celery looks like carrots. They grow large turnips for cow-feed (weigh about 4 lbs.) They also have purple cabbage but I guess that's not too unusual.

Can't tell yet when I'll be home. I'll have to change my guess on when I'll be home from August 15 to, let's say last of Nov. I should be home the last of Nov. Of course something could happen and I could make it before then.

All my love,
Cecil

Putting off the next transport of troops made the Army as unpopular as a doctor that changes an anxious would-be mother's due date. Every soldier was counting the days and must have tried to be patient because they knew their time was coming. The Army would not leave them in Europe forever. However, the days seemed to drag on and on in the interim.

August 6, 1945
Landa, Germany

Dearest Mom and Dad,

I received your letter of July 26 and I'm glad everyone is OK.

Wish I could tell you I'm coming home but I can't. Don't know a thing about when it will be yet.

Yes, I know I should be patient over here and not complain about the things that can't be helped. Actually, I'm not worried about the things that can't be helped. It's the things that could be helped. Right here in my division there are men with less points than I have already in the process of going home.

You two can never know what the life of a soldier is like over here now. I will just mention a little incident that happened here. The other day the Sergeant asked me to drive a jeep for about 20 minutes. It turned out that I barely had time to eat supper and I had to drive a Colonel and a Captain to a nearby town to attend a party given by the division commander. There were four generals present and about 15 other officers. They had nurses, WAC's, or Red Cross girls with them. I arrived at 7 o'clock and waited out in front till 1:30 in the morning then brought them back. I'm just the type of fellow that think people are created equal. I could never get used to a sergeant waiting on a colonel for 6 ½ hours while he danced and drank liquor.

Well, don't worry. I'm OK just don't like the ways of the army–just like a few million other fellows.

Yes, there were 15 guns in all. They may confiscate my radio before it gets home.

So long. Goodnight–Lovingly,
Cecil

Newt must have admonished his son for the letter complaining about things in the Army that couldn't be helped. Cecil gave a quick story of one incident that was unnecessary and cemented his opinion of the Army way. Like so many average Joe Americans, Cecil was unacquainted with ranks and other aspects of military life before the war. After the GI's served their duty and the world was safe once again, most had a new appreciation of being a classless civilian and would never own another green garment. Following the war, Cecil never cared for boiled chicken which he quickly dismissed as "Army chicken!"

Aug 9, 1945
Landa, Germany

Dearest Mom and Dad,

Your letter of July 30 came today and it was one of the best because you talked Dad into writing also.

I wish I had been home for your birthday, Mom, but there are those who are much worse off than I am.

Don't know when I'll be home. If you see fellows at home who have about 90 points and fought over here with us don't think anything about it. That's one of the usual ways the Army messes things up.

I was going to be in favor of a permanent draft when the war was over but the last 3 months has changed my mind.

No, Dad, I have not forgotten the promise the Lord made you that I would come home from the war. I have been thru close ones and thought that my time had come but thru some act of the Lord I lived thru it all. I sometimes thought I was living on borrowed time. Last nite I lay awake in the big guard house and prayed for everyone I know and all the troubled world. The house was quiet. I was the only one in it. We sleep there when we are on guard. We soldiers have a bad habit of calling on the Lord when we are in a tight place and forget Him when the sailing is good. Always remember me in your prayers.

The news of Russia declaring war and the new atom bomb is good. I only hope the new bomb scares the Japs into surrendering and the world never needs it again. It is almost impossible to imagine the power of it.

Goodnight. Say Hello to all!

All my love,
Cecil

    Sgt. Turner recognized many insights and valuable lessons he had learned the past four years. He had seen the same growth in others as well and thought at one time that all young men would benefit from the same experience. Cecil had watched the war-time military change drastically after VE Day and changed his mind. The longer he stayed in Europe, the worse his opinion became.

Newt had reminded his son in the last letter from home that God had kept His promise that Cecil would be coming home to him. Through many close calls, Deacon Turner could see the hand of God intervening in a miraculous way. Cecil knew the power of prayer had pulled him through and was faithful to call on the same power on behalf of all his friends, loved ones, and the world. He had been in the center of the turmoil during some of our planet's darkest hours. Cecil knew how God must weep over His creation and asked for intervention and guidance as these war-torn countries tried to pick up the pieces. In his letter, he confessed his prayers were more fervent from the foxholes, but was trying to rectify that by continuing to call on his God now that the crises had passed.

The short statements about Russia and the atomic bomb are living history as the two seemed to be the final blows to end the war. Even in Germany, Cecil and other soldiers were joining the world in awe of the power released on Japan and hoping it would never need to be used again.

Aug 14, 1945
Landa, Germany

Dearest Mom & Dad & Ava,

Hurray! The mail got through today and I got 7 letters. Yours, Mom, was dated Aug. 3 and, Ava, yours was dated Aug. 2.

It tickles me pink to hear that all guns are there now and my radio. I was sure waiting to hear from the radio. There are two large meters yet, the only things that I can't account for. They may be there now.

The war may be over now for all I know. There's supposed to be an announcement at 4 o'clock and it's after 4 now. This is supposed to be my birthday I believe. Sure wish it would end today. Good present no? I might be home a little sooner if the war is over now.

Ava, you ask who the girl was in the picture. I take for granted that you mean the picture under the glass. She is a girl in Reading, Pa. Back in Italy her cousin who is a very good friend of mine asked me to write to his cousin. I did and she later sent me all of the pictures. That's the story. She writes nice letters and I hope to see her someday.

I have a new job now. A friend of mine, Mike Kopanski, and I each night go to one of the three battalions that are in our artillery and show them a movie. We use a small Army moving picture machine and a small generator driven by a gasoline motor. Tonite we go to a little town, Boxburg. We will show it there in the school house. It takes us about thirty minutes to get set up each night. We pull a trailer, which has the motor mounted in it. It's not a bad job. Last nite we showed "The Affair of Susan" to the 862nd Field Artillery Battalion.

This is the next day and the war was over last nite. Some of the boys came in last nite about 3:00 and woke me up to tell me the news. We have been expecting it a long time now. Everyone is very happy of course.

I'll go eat super. Love,
Cecil

Cecil (left) and Mike Kopanski drive movie truck with equipment to entertain other batteries in the area. (August, 1945)

News was slow to arrive in Landa concerning the Pacific war ending on August 14, 1945. Although Cecil's sister had confused him, his birthday was on the 13th and VJ Day would always be celebrated the day after. This marked the fifth birthday he had spent in the military.

He seemed to like his new job better perhaps because the units would have welcomed the sight of Turner's truck coming. Entertaining bored men was more rewarding than the guard post assignment.

Aug. 18, 1945
Dearest Mom & Dad,

Here I am still in Landa, Germany and doing OK. I have just returned from Boxburg where we showed one of the battalions a moving picture.

Maybe you had better not send me any more mail–maybe we will be moving over into France pretty soon–and if you wrote more letters I might not get them anyway.

I received your letter of August 10 and it was the only one I got today which made it worth twice as much.

I read where your ration is lifted and that a half million cars will be made by Jan. 1st.

That's all folks! Can't wait to see you!

Hello everybody. Love,
Cecil

With the Japanese conflict over, troops in Germany hoped that would speed their return home as well. Turner was not the only soldier caught in the red tape that seemed to complicate the occupational experience.

The end of the war brought a change in category and alerted the 36th for shipment home. Wholesale shifting of troops from one division to another accompanied redeployment preparations, not once, but several times. There were many delays, all of them in turn sorrowfully lamented by the waiting men . . . [34]

The renewed optimism that perhaps VJ Day and shuffling units would expedite their transport home would be short-lived. Cecil had his hopes raised and would come down hard when disappointed again.

The soldiers were inundated with rumors and misinformation. All this led to long faces every time the rumors turned out wrong and the days of occupation dragged on. If good news wasn't coming from Headquarters, at least some was coming from home. The lifting of rations meant that life was getting back to normal at home and Cecil would be a part of that "normality" soon.

August 26, 1945
Landa, Germany

Dearest Mom & Dad,

I believe I have received two letters from you since I have answered. I am OK and still with the 63rd.

I have told you not to write because I think I will have a new address before I would receive any more mail. Please don't expect me home soon though but if you consider this good news I'll say that I should see you by Oct. 1st. I really believe that I will be home by then but to me that is a long way off. I don't get enthused anymore over that kind of news. I don't think the Army could surprise or disappoint me anymore. Don't get the idea that I'm all in the "dumps." It's just that I have been led to believe so many times that it wouldn't be long now.

I'll write again from other spots in France.

All my love,
Cecil

Sgt. Turner knew his family wanted and expected to hear from him, but it was hard to find anything to say. They were waiting for news on when he could come home, but he was caught in the same waiting pattern. He decided it was surely safe to say he would be home by October although he cringed at the idea of being in Germany until then. It is unfortunate the Army could not provide better coordination and communication leaving Cecil with a positive last impression.

August 28, 1945
Landa, Germany

Dearest Mom & Dad,

This afternoon finds me doing fine and not doing a thing. I may have "jumped the gun" on my guess again. I must never believe anything anymore. I could be home by Oct. 1st but I don't know.

Don't ever believe anything you hear about us coming home. I believe they announced that we would be on our way home within 30 days after V-J day. We won't! The only other prediction I care to make is maybe before Christmas.

I have been over here so long that I guess a few more weeks won't matter. I'll be very happy when I do get home and see you all.

God bless you,

Lovingly,
Cecil

The previous two letters, written just two days apart, demonstrate the lack of reliable information to the weary soldier. In the first quick note, the October arrival date was fairly certain. Two days later, even that is thrown out. The strain in Cecil's usual positive attitude was easy to detect in the August letters which echoed the frustration of the constant delays he was enduring.

Sept 8, 1945
Camp Lucky Strike

Dearest Mom and Dad,

I have at last begun the slow process of getting ready to come home. I don't know when it will be yet but not too long off. I'm here in France now. I might be on my way in two weeks.

I'm not too far from Le Harve the French port.

I'm still mourning a number of my old friends—ones I have known for 3–4 years.

I will try to write again while I'm here at Camp Lucky Strike. Don't write. I would never get it.

Love,
Cecil

Finally, the letter his family had waited so long for arrived. Cecil was coming home! Ten days after the previous gloomy letter, Cecil was already in France and preparing for his trip to the U.S. He was located at one of a cluster of temporary bases processing troops home from all over Europe. His camp, appropriately named

"Lucky Strike," was near Le Havre, France, on the English Channel. Processing and transportation would take three weeks, but at least things were moving in the right direction—home!

Before boarding a ship, Cecil had time to reflect on his years in Europe. What occupied his mind the most was "a number of his old friends." He had spent 3–4 years of his life with these men in the most critical situations. Too many of his "fox-hole buddies" were not going home, but occupied graves marking the path of the Texans. Due to attrition, captures, injuries, and deaths, the T-Patchers, by the end of the war, barely resembled the group that had congregated at Camp Bowie in 1941. Sgt. Turner was part of only 10% out of the original 11,000 Texans who would be boarding ships for home. Over the course of the war, just over 30,000 men were attached to the T-Patchers with almost 17,000 listed as casualties. The 36th Division ranked 9th highest in the number of casualties of all American Divisions in WW II. In this last letter, Cecil finally acknowledged the loss he felt and spent his last days on European soil mourning freedom's costly price in young lives.

Cecil is ready to head back home. 1945

(telegram)

Sept 29, 1945

Arrived Norfolk Virginia today be in San Antonio soon for discharge will call you then love.

Cecil 505 pm

Two and a half years earlier, before he sailed toward the war, Cecil urged his family, "Always remember me when you talk to the Lord and I'll be coming home some day." That day had finally come.

His official discharge came on October 8th, 1945. Cecil had contributed more than four of the best years in a young man's life in service to his country. According to the family, Cecil's exact time and date of arrival were unclear. Some of them were at the local movie theater when Cecil found them. He hid in the back seat of the car while they drove up to his brother Hubert's home. When they asked his sister-in-law, Georgia, if she would like to see Cecil, she replied, "Of course!" When he popped up, she almost fainted. That night the family feasted on a coming-home meal that included a big bowl of mashed potatoes, embellished with green peas spelling out "Cecil," and, of course, a heaping plate of fried chicken.

EPILOGUE

★ ★ ★ ★ ★

And the Lord will deliver me from every evil work and preserve me for His heavenly kingdom. To him be glory for ever and ever. Amen!

II Timothy 4:18 (NKJV)

Cecil's prayer to return to the farm was answered when he came back to Nolan County, Texas. He began to work the soil that had been such a part of his life and was waiting for him upon his return. Life was good and returning to normal when friends introduced him to a nurse in nearby Sweetwater. Kathleen Freeman had recently come home from nursing school in Tennessee. On February 8, 1948, 30 year-old Cecil took Kathleen as his wife. Newt Turner's brother, Henry, was a minister who held the ceremony in his home in Abilene, Texas with the families gathered around. They prayed God's blessings on these two who had found each other after losing years and dear friends to the war.

Cecil takes his bride back to the Hotel Ponce De Leon in St. Augustine, Florida for their honeymoon. (February, 1948)

For their honeymoon, Cecil took his new bride to St. Augustine, Florida, just as he had vowed eight years earlier when impressed by the beautiful, historic city. Two years and two children later, the young family moved to an irrigated farm near Hale Center, Texas. Cecil's brother, Hubert, had moved up on the South Plains a short time earlier and convinced his younger brother to follow. They formed a partnership, Turner Brothers Land Company, to sell farm real estate and work their own farms as well. Kathleen settled in with daughter Viki, and son Eddie (Cecil Edwin Turner Jr.). Before the year 1951 ended, another daughter, Kathie, was added and Cecil returned to Roscoe to bury his father, weakened from heart disease. In 1956, Cecil's family was complete with the birth of daughter, Terri.

By 1956, Cecil and Kathleen have four children:
clockwise from left; Viki, Eddie, Kathie, and Terri.

"Mr. Turner" at home in his civilian clothes

In the 1950's, Cecil, right, formed his second partnership with brother Hubert to start a real estate business, Turner Brothers Land Company in Hale Center, Texas. The brothers continued to farm as well.

The family flourished on the farm and in the local Baptist church. Cecil raised his children to love the Lord as he had been raised. He sang in the choir and he and Kathleen taught Sunday School. "Deacon" became a ministry instead of a nickname after Cecil was ordained. Worship and fellowship in the local church was an opportunity he was going to take advantage of for himself and his family, a lesson learned in his travels while in the military.

Cecil on his farm near Hale Center in the 1970's

Army buddies stayed in touch with Christmas cards and occasional visits. Cecil would at times discuss his war experience, but rarely spoke of any difficult memories. He joined the 36th Division Alumni Association but eventually would let his membership lapse. The cascading years of civilian life caused his war encounter to fade as pleasant and painful memories faded. At times, his military service must have seemed like a dream—so foreign from his life before and since. When his children were grown, however, he wanted them to know the truth of the Holocaust and showed them the pictures.

Cecil and Kathleen in the 1970's.

Cecil with six of his nine grandchildren in 1984

Cecil had prostate problems that he traced back to years of bumpy rides in Army jeeps and trucks. Even with frequent check-ups, he developed prostate cancer in 1981 that soon spread to his bones. Deacon Turner was at war again and put up a good fight. He and Kathleen made the most of those last years together and traveled to see the Cape Cod area he had fallen in love with while at Camp Edwards. In 1985, however, it was clear that he was losing the battle and soon would be going to see his Lord. With just a few months to live, he went to several friends for whom he prayed many years. Cecil's "death bed" witness of the truths of the Bible and the abundant life for believers here and beyond led thirteen of these friends to join him in his faith in Christ. As these and other friends gathered with Kathleen and children at Cecil's funeral in February 1986, it was a bittersweet occasion. All four children loved the same God as their grandfather Newt, and were raising Cecil's nine grandchildren to follow Christ as well. To look at the brief inscription on the Army headstone was another reminder of the life devoted to God as a farm boy, spared in a war on foreign soil, and blessed as an adult.

Cecil Edwin Turner
Tec 4 US Army
World War II
Aug 13 1918-Feb 9 1986

I have fought a good fight, I have finished my course, I have kept the faith . .

(2 Timothy 4:7, KJV)

Chemotherapy was taking its toll on Cecil in the spring of 1985. Daughters Kathie (left) and Terri pose with their parents (Cecil wears a hat to cover his lack of hair).

Letter to Cecil

Dear Daddy,

My children suggested I write you this letter to complete this book of your letters. How proud you would be of them and your other six grandchildren. Your many prayers for them have been answered as they are becoming godly adults and starting families of their own. How much I want them to know of your faith in Christ and for the godly heritage you fought to preserve and lived to exemplify. "Thank you" seems so inadequate to describe the overwhelming debt of gratitude we owe: for the years of youth that you forfeited for our freedoms, for the life you lived before us, for your love, and for your prayers—Oh, your prayers: so unrehearsed, honest and personal. All who heard them felt we were eavesdropping on a very personal conversation between two who were accustomed to this type of intimacy. I asked you to pray at my wedding because I knew God would be there if you were going to talk to Him. The Bible tells us that all our requests are still being offered up at God's throne of grace. What peace and strength it gives me to know your umbrella of prayers are still with me.

While questioning God's slowness in answering our prayers for your healing, I asked you why God had not acted. Your answer put aside my doubts as you reminded me that we were not God, and thankfully so. How often we would mess up His plans if God gave in to our every desire, even those outside His purpose for us. God did not show you why healing did not come, but continued to wrap His arms around you with a Peace that carried you through the days ahead. I recall the day your body gave out and released you for heaven to be with the Lord. I heard you calling His names: Jehovah, Abba, Adoni . . . and knew the communication would continue face to face.

I long to share a mansion with you and worship beside you again,

Kathie Lou

> *Only be careful, and watch yourselves closely so that you do not forget the things your eyes have seen or let them slip from your heart as long as you live. Teach them to your children and to their children after them.*
>
> (Deuteronomy 4: 9, NIV)

NOTES

Chapter 2

1. Sorin F, Gardening the Founding Father's Way. USA Weekend, 2004 July 2–4, 10.

Chapter 3

1. United States Army, The Story of the 36th Infantry Division, (Paris, France: Desfosse-Neogravure, no date recorded—immediate postwar), 3.

2. Ibid, 4.

3. Ibid.

4. The 36th Division Association, A Pictorial History of the 36th Division, (Austin,   c. 1945) no page numbers.

5. Official After Action Reports, 36th Infantry Division, National Archives, Information Section, Analysis Branch, Headquarters Army Ground Force, Washington 25, D. C., 1 March 1947. microfilm records in the Texas State Archives, no page numbers.

6. Turner C, A Service at the Front, Baptist Standard, 20 April 1944(used by permission) 13.

7. U. S. Army, 6.

8. Ibid.

9. Official Report.

10. Daily News – New York City, 24 November 1943 (used by permission of Daily News and Associated Press, article retyped and included in the Official After Action Reports in the National Archives) 59.

11. Falmouth News, 1943 (used by permission, article retyped and included in the Official After Action Reports in the National Archives).

12. 36th Division.

13. Ibid.

14. After Action Reports.

15. 36th Division.

16. After Action Reports.

17. Ibid.

18. 36th Division.

19. U. S. Army, 11-12.

Chapter 4

1. 36th Division.

2. U.S. Army, 12.

3. Lockart, V, T-Patch to Victory (Canyon: Staked Plains Press, 1981), 16.

4. 36th Division.

5. Ibid.

6. After Action Reports.

7. 36th Division.

8. Lockart, 93.

9. Ibid, 95.

10. Ibid, 96-97.

11. Ibid, 107.

12. U.S. Army, 17.

13. 36th Division.

14. Lockart, 114.

15. Ibid. 132.

16. 36th Division.

17. Ibid.

18. Ibid.

19. Ibid.

20. Ibid.

21. Ibid.

22. U. S. Army, 21.

23. 36th Division.

24. Ibid.

25. Lockart, 161.

26. Ibid, 171.

27. Ibid.

28. 36th Division.

29. Ibid.

30. U. S. Army, 23.

31. 36th Division.

32. U. S. Army, 23.

33. Ibid, 25.

34. Lockart, 214.

35. Ibid. 215.

36. Ibid.

37. 36th Division.

38. Lockart, 225.

39. Ibid, 237.

40. Ibid, 239

Chapter 5

1. 36th Division.

2. Lockart, 261.

3. After Action Reports.

4. 36th Division.

5. After Action Reports.

6. 36th Division.

7. Ibid.

8. Ibid.

9. Ibid.

10. Lockart, 273.

11. 36th Division.

12. Lockart, 273.

13. Ibid

14. 36th Division.

15. Ibid.

16. Lockart, 275-276.

17. Ibid, 277-278.

18. Ibid, 276.

19. Ibid, 277.

20. Ibid, 282.

21. Ibid.

22. Ibid, 280.

23. Ibid.

24. 36th Division.

25. Ibid.

26. Lockart, 286.

27. Ibid.

28. After Action Reports.

29. 36th Division.

30. Ibid.

31. Lockart, 267.

32. Ibid, 269-270.

33. 36th Division.

34. Ibid.

CREDITS

★ ★ ★ ★ ★

"Official After Action Reports, 36th Division" microfilm records in the Texas State Archives, Information Section, Analysis Branch, Headquarters Army Ground Force, Washington 25, D. C., March 1, 1947.

The 36th Division Association. A Pictorial History of the 36th Division: Austin, c. 1945.

United States Army. The Story of the 36th Infantry Division, Desfosse-Neogravure, Paris, c. 1945.

Fran Sorin, "Gardening the Founding Father's Way," USA Weekend, (July 2–4, 2004): 10.

Turner, Cecil. "A Service at the Front," Baptist Standard, (April 20, 1944): 13.

Lockhart Vincent, T-Patch To Victory. Canyon, TX: Staked Plains Press, 1981.

Five Years—Five Countries—Five Campaigns. An account of the 141st Infantry in World War II published by the 141st Regiment Association in Munich, Germany, 1945. Edited by Clifford H. Peek, Jr.

Contact author Kathie Jackson
or order more copies of this book at

TATE PUBLISHING, LLC

127 East Trade Center Terrace
Mustang, Oklahoma 73064

(888) 361 - 9473

Tate Publishing, LLC